BIRMINGHAM RE
IN ASSOCIATION WITH THE ROYAL COURT PRE...

BY GURPREET KAUR BHATTI

Commissioned by Birmingham Repertory Theatre
First performed at The STUDIO,
Birmingham Repertory Theatre on 22 May 2014

CAST

JEETO	Sudha Bhuchar
LIZ	Lauren Crace
MAJOR	Neil D'Souza
REEMA	Preeya Kalidas
PAL	Rez Kempton
COOKIE	Zita Sattar

CREATIVES

Writer	Gurpreet Kaur Bhatti
Director	Roxana Silbert
Designer	Jamie Vartan
Lighting Designer	Chahine Yavroyan
Sound Designer	Giles Thomas
Visual & Projection Designer	Nathan Jones
Casting Director	Julia Horan CDG
Assistant Director	Erin Gilley
Voice & Dialect Coach	Zabarjad Salam
Design Assistant	Gayatri Jani
Stage Manager	Ruth Morgan
Deputy Stage Manager	Juliette Taylor
Assistant Stage Manager	Hannan Finnegan

Paint supplied by Farrow & Ball Solihull Showroom
Thank You to ASDA Capehill

Sudha Bhuchar Jeeto
Theatre credits include: *Strictly Dandia* and *A Fine Balance* (Tamasha Theatre Company); *Haroun And The Sea Of Stories* (National Theatre) and *A Yearning* (Birmingham Repertory Theatre). Film credits include: *All In Good Time* (Leftbank Pictures). Television credits include: *Stella* (Tidy Productions) and *Murder, Doctors, Holby City, Casualty* and *EastEnders* (BBC). Radio credits include: *An Everyday Story Of Afghan Folk, Behind the Beautiful Forevers, Silver Street* and *The Archers* (BBC). Sudha is also a playwright and her current work includes *My Name Is...* at the Arcola.

Lauren Crace Liz
Lauren trained at RADA. Her theatre credits include: *Theatre Uncut* (Young Vic); *And I And Silence* (Finborough Theatre) and *Les Liaisons Dangereuses* (Salisbury Playhouse). Television credits include: *Mr Selfridge* series 1, 2 and 3 (ITV); *Room At The Top, Holby City, Silk, Sherlock: The Great Game* and *Eastenders* (BBC) and *Shameless* (Channel 4). Radio credits include: *The Martin Beck Killings* (BBC Radio 4) and *Minister Of Chance* (Radio Static). Other work includes: *Skyvers* (National Theatre) and *Spur Of The Moment* (Royal Court). Lauren won Best Newcomer at the TV Choice/TV Quick Awards 2009.

Neil D'Souza Major
Theatre credits include: *Drawing The Line* (Hampstead Theatre); *Much Ado About Nothing, Midnight's Children* (Royal Shakespeare Company); *Tintin* (West End and No.1 tour); *The Man of Mode* (National Theatre); *Twelfth Night* (West End); *Merchant of Venice, The Honest Whore* (Shakespeare's Globe); *Skeleton* (Soho Theatre). Television credits include: *Friday Night Dinner* (Big Talk); *Doctors, Holby City* (BBC); *Hustle* (Kudos) and *The Bill* (Thames TV). Film credits include: *Still Life* (Fox); *Closed Circuit* (Working Title); *Filth* (Steel Mill Films); *Italian Movies* (Indiana). Radio credits include *Goan Flame* and *The Red Oleander* (BBC). Work as a writer includes: *Small Miracle* (Tricycle Theatre), *Five Beats To The Bar* (Radio 4), *Westway* (World Service), *The Bollywoods* (BBC). He is currently commissioned to write a stage play for the Watford Palace Theatre.

Preeya Kalidas Reema
Theatre credits include: *Oxford Street* (Royal Court); *Bombay Dreams* (Apollo Victoria) and *Joseph And His Amazing Technicolor Dreamcoat* (Adelphi Theatre). Television credits include: *EastEnders, Mistresses, Bodies, My Family* and *Hotel Babylon* (BBC); *Bollywood Carmen* (BBC3); *Mr Eleven* (Tiger Aspect); *Britz* (Mentorn/Channel 4) and *Decreed* (HTV West). Film credits include: *Four Lions* (Warp Films); *It's A Wonderful Afterlife* (Bend it Films); *Bend It Like Beckham* (Rock Media); *East Is East* (East Is East Productions); *Jump Boy* (Dancing Fleas Productions); *Sari And Trainers* (Stretch Limo Productions) and *The Fiancée* (Minerva Films).

Rez Kempton Pal
Theatre credits include:
Transmissions and *Nativity*
(Birmingham Repertory Theatre);
Drawing The Line (Hampstead
Theatre); *The Battle of Green
Lanes* (Theatre Royal Stratford
East); *Arrange That Marriage*
(UK Tour); *Heer Ranjha* (mac,
Birmingham). Television credits
include: *Adha Cup* and *Singapore
Mutiny* (Channel 4); *Doctors,
Trial By Jury* and *Roger Roger*
(BBC); *The Bill* and *Fall* (ITV).
Radio credits include: *Silver
Street* and *The Raj Quartet*
(BBC). Film credits include:
Amar Akbar & Tony (Sash
Media Productions); *Chakara*
(Laid Back Films), *Life Goes On*
(Stormglass Productions) and *The
Mystic Masseur* (Merchant Ivory
Productions).

Zita Sattar Cookie
Theatre credits include: *East
Is East* (Birmingham Repertory
Theatre/Royal Court); *Silence*
(Birmingham Repertory Theatre);
Top Girls (Northampton Theatre
Royal); *Romeo & Juliet* (Leicester
Haymarket); *A Yearning* (Tamasha
Tour); *Precious* and *Seeds Under
Stones* (West Yorkshire Playhouse)
and *D'yer Eat With Your Fingers?!*
(Stratford East).Television
credits include: *According To
Bex, Casualty, Heartburn Hotel,
Gimme Gimme Gimme* and
Prisoners' Wives (BBC) and *Love
Life* (ITV). Film credits include:
Another Me (Rainy Day Films);
West is West (BBC Films); *Janice
Beard 45wpm* (Dakota Films);
Esther Kahn (Magic Lantern
Films); *Large* (Film Four) and
Almost Adult (Bankside Films).

Gurpreet Kaur Bhatti Writer
Gurpreet Kaur Bhatti has written
extensively for stage, screen and
radio. Her first play *Behsharam
(Shameless)* broke box office
records at Soho Theatre and
the Birmingham Repertory
Theatre in 2001. Her play *Behzti
(Dishonour)* was sensationally
closed in December 2004, after
playing to packed houses at The
REP. In 2005, *Behzti* won the
Susan Smith Blackburn Prize and
in 2006, the play was translated
into French and did sell-out tours
in France and Belgium. *Behzti*
was translated into Italian in 2012
and was performed in Bari, Italy.
In 2010 her follow up to *Behzti
– Behud (Beyond Belief)* was
co-produced by Soho Theatre
and Coventry Belgrade and
shortlisted for the John Whiting
Award. Other credits include the
British feature, *Everywhere And
Nowhere, DCI Stone* (Radio 4),
Londonee (Rich Mix), *Dead Meat*
(Channel 4) and *An Enemy Of The
People* (BBC World Service). Her
play for Watford Palace Theatre,
Fourteen, will also be produced
this May. She is currently under
commission to the National
Theatre and is a member of the
writing team of *The Archers*.

Roxana Silbert Director
Roxana is Artistic Director of
Birmingham Repertory Theatre
and was an Associate Director of
the Royal Shakespeare Company.
Roxana was Artistic Director of
Paines Plough Theatre Company
(2005-2009); Literary Director
at the Traverse Theatre (2001-
2004) and Associate Director,
Royal Court (1998-2000). In

1997, Roxana was Associate Director of the West Yorkshire Playhouse. Recent credits include *Dunsinane* (National Theatre of Scotland and Royal Shakespeare Company); *A Life of Galileo* (Royal Shakespeare Company and Birmingham Repertory Theatre) and *Tartuffe* (Birmingham Repertory Theatre).

Jamie Vartan Designer
Jamie Vartan is an award-winning designer, his current theatre credits include: *Ballyturk* (Galway Arts Festival 2014 and National Theatre). Previous theatre credits include: *Misterman* (Galway Arts Festival 2011, National Theatre and St Anne's Warehouse, New York); *The Hostage, Mrs Warren's Profession* and *The Playboy of the Western World* (National Theatre of Ireland) and *Mass Observation* (Almeida Theatre). Current work in opera includes: *Romeo et Juliette* (Herceg Novi Amphitheatre, Montenegro) and *Manon Lescaut* (Palau de les Arts Reina Sofia, Valencia). His design for *A Village Romeo and Juliet* (Wexford Operai) won the Irish Times Best Set Design Award 2013.

Chahine Yavroyan
Lighting Designer
Theatre credits include: *Tartuffe, Have Box Will Travel* and *Orphans* (Birmingham Repertory Theatre); *King Lear, Major Barbara* (The Abbey, Dublin); *Fuente Ovejuna* (Teatros del Canal, Madrid); *Three Sisters, A Comedy of Errors* (Manchester Royal Exchange); *Let The Right One In, The Pass, Narrative,* *Relocated* and *Wig Out!* (Royal Court); *The Vortex* (The Gate, Dublin); *Fall, Damascus* and *When The Bulbul Stopped Singing* (Traverse Theatre); *Mahabharata* (Sadler's Wells); *Dallas Sweetman, House of Agnes* (Paines Plough).

Giles Thomas Sound Designer
Composer/Sound Designer credits include: *Prime Time, Untitled Matriarch Play, Mint* and *Pigeons* (Royal Court); *Take A Deep Breath and Breathe* (Oval House Theatre) and *Stop Kiss* (Leicester Square Theatre). Sound Designer credits include: *Superior Donuts* (Southwark Playhouse); *Three Men In a Boat* (Original Theatre Company, UK Tour); *Shoot/Get Treasure/ Repeat* and *House of Agnes* (Paines Plough). Associate Sound Designer credits include: *Henry V* (Michael Grandage Company). Music Producer credits include: *An Appointment with the Wickerman* (National Theatre Scotland).

Nathan Jones Visual & Projection Designer
Nat Jones (aka Soopanatural) worked recently with Birmingham Repertory Theatre to create the visuals for *The Legend Of Mike Smith*, Soweto Kinch's theatre production directed by Jonzi D. Other artistic collaborations have included Nike, Akala, Charlie Dark, Mark De Clive-Lowe, Boy Blue Entertainment, Brighton Hip Hop Festival and Nu Century Arts. Soopanatural Productions' work has featured on BBC, at London's Queen Elizabeth Hall,

Royal Festival Hall, the Tate Modern, The REP, The Albany, Copenhagen Jazz Festival, York Jazz Festival, Cargo in Shoreditch, XOYO in London, The Wardrobe in Leeds, the Rome Coliseum and numerous other theatre venues, music festivals and clubs in Europe. Current projects include Lapetus Records (South Africa), *The Legend Of Mike Smith* and The Hip Hop Shakespeare Company's production of *Richard II* which was at the Southbank Centre earlier this year.

Julia Horan CDG Casting Director
Theatre includes: *The Nether, Adler & Gibb, Birdland, The Mistress Contract, Gastronauts, Clybourne Park, Wanderlust* and *Sucker Punch* (Royal Court); *A View from the Bridge, Happy Days* and *A Doll's House* (West End/BAM); *After Miss Julie, The Glass Menagerie* and *Annie Get Your Gun* (Young Vic); *Mr Burns, Chimerica, Through a Glass Darkly, Measure for Measure* and *The Homecoming* (Almeida); *The Events, A Brief History of Helen of Troy* (ATC); *Spring Awakening, The Seagull* (Headlong); *Another Country* (CFT/West End); *A Chorus of Disapproval, Absent Friends, As You Like It* and *The Weir* (West End); *Gaddafi: A Living Myth* (English National Opera); *Othello* (Cheek by Jowl). Television includes: *Adha Cup, Parliamo Glasgow, Harvest* (IWC Media); *The*

Verdict (Lionsgate Television); *The Bill* (Thames Television); *The Badness of George IV* (Flashback Television). Film includes: *Puffins*.

Erin Gilley Assistant Director
Previous assistant director credits at Birmingham Repertory Theatre include: *Twelve Angry Men* and *A Life of Galileo*. She is currently the Artistic Director of elastic future and was also the Artistic Producer of Magic Theatre in San Francisco. Most recently she directed the digital theatre performance *Peek A Boo* for LIFT. Other credits include: *The Unauthorized Autobiography of Kim Deal* and *Beautiful* (elastic future); *Wreckage* (Crowded Fire) and *Equus* (Boxcar Theatre). Erin studied theatre as an undergraduate at Princeton University and is currently on secondment at Birmingham Repertory Theatre as a Birkbeck MFA candidate.

Zabarjad Salam Voice & Dialect Coach
Theatre credits include: *We Are Proud to Present* (Bush); *Other Desert Cities* (Old Vic); *Once a Catholic* (Tricycle); *The Djinns of Eidgah* (Royal Court); *Sizwe Bansi is Dead* (Young Vic); *The Commitments, Let It Be* (West End); *Julius Caesar, The Winter's Tale, Matilda* and *Much Ado About Nothing* (Royal Shakespeare Company); *Goodnight Mr Tom* (Chichester Festival); *The Veil, 13, The Comedy of Errors, Travelling Light,*

Collaborators, The Last of the Haussmans, Timon of Athens and *This House* (National Theatre); *Zaide* (Sadler's Wells/ UK tour). Television includes: *Being Eileen, Blandings* (BBC); *Cucumber, Indian Summers* (Channel 4) and *Cilla* (ITV).

Gayatri Jani Design Assistant Gayatri Jani is a designer with a multitude of skills, from her early background in Graphic Design, to a degree in Product Design bringing in the 3D world. Her true passion remained on stage and she continued this in her spare time. Her experience in 2D and 3D design has led her to creating and dressing scenery, props and images for live performances and short films. Gayatri is a highly experienced design assistant and her credits include: *Women Of Hope* – promotional material; *October Wild Card* (Sadler's Wells) – set designer; *Brood or Thought* (short film) – production designer; *Michael Jackson 51* (Curve Theatre) – props and promotional material.

Birmingham Repertory Theatre is one of Britain's leading producing theatre companies. Founded in 1913 by Sir Barry Jackson, Birmingham Repertory Theatre Company rapidly became one of the most famous and exciting theatre companies in the country launching the careers of an array of many great British actors including Laurence Olivier, Ralph Richardson, Edith Evans, Paul Scofield, Derek Jacobi, Elizabeth Spriggs, Albert Finney and many more. In 2013 the company celebrated its centenary.

The theatre's programme includes many premieres from new versions of the classics to contemporary writing. The commissioning and production of new work lies at the core of The REP's programme and over the last 15 years the company has produced more than 130 new plays.

Many of The REP's productions go on to have lives beyond Birmingham transferring to the West End and touring nationally and internationally. Recent transfers and tours include *Twelve Angry Men* at the Garrick Theatre, Philip Pullman's *I Was A Rat!* and Kate Tempest's *Hopelessly Devoted*.

The REP's long-running production of *The Snowman* recently celebrated its 20th anniversary. It has become a must-see fixture in London's West End calendar, playing to packed houses at the Peacock Theatre every Christmas for the last 15 years. *The Snowman* also tours regularly across the UK and to theatres in Holland, Korea, Japan and Finland.

The REP re-opened in Autumn 2013 following a two-and-a-half year refurbishment alongside the new Library of Birmingham. The refurbishment of the theatre includes a new 300-seat studio theatre as well as the restoration of its original façade, plus much improved public and backstage facilities.

Artistic Director Roxana Silbert
Executive Director Stuart Rogers

Box Office: 0121 236 4455
Administration: 0121 245 2000
birmingham-rep.co.uk

Birmingham Repertory Theatre is a registered charity, number 223660

Supported using public funding by
ARTS COUNCIL ENGLAND

NOW IS THE TIME TO ACT

ACT ONE   ACT TWO   DOUBLE ACT   FAMILY ACT

Join The REP's ACT membership scheme today and receive a range of great benefits such as priority booking, discounts and invites to special events. Our membership schemes are an excellent way for you to support The REP whilst getting some fantastic benefits for yourself.

For more information or to buy one of our memberships, visit **birmingham-rep.co.uk** or call our Box Office, The BOX, on **0121 236 4455**.

THE ENGLISH STAGE COMPANY
AT THE ROYAL COURT THEATRE

The Royal Court is the writers' theatre. It is a leading force in world theatre, finding writers and producing new plays that are original and contemporary. The Royal Court strives to be at the centre of civic, political, domestic and international life, giving writers a home to tackle big ideas and world events and tell great stories.

photo: Stephen Cummiskey

The Royal Court commissions and develops an extraordinary quantity of new work, reading over 3000 scripts a year and annually producing around 14 world or UK premieres in its two auditoria at Sloane Square in London. Over 200,000 people visit the Royal Court each year and many thousands more see our work elsewhere through transfers to the West End and New York, national and international tours, residencies across London and site-specific work, including recent Theatre Local Seasons in Peckham, King's Cross and Haggerston.

The Royal Court's extensive development activity encompasses a diverse range of writers and artists and includes an ongoing programme of writers' attachments, readings, workshops and playwriting groups. Twenty years of pioneering work around the world means the Royal Court has relationships with writers on every continent.

The Royal Court opens its doors to radical thinking and provocative discussion, and to the unheard voices and free thinkers that, through their writing, change our way of seeing.

"With its groundbreaking premieres and crusading artistic directors, the Royal Court has long enjoyed a reputation as one of our most daring, seat-of-its-pants theatres." The Times

"The most important theatre in Europe." New York Times

Within the past sixty years, John Osborne, Arnold Wesker and Howard Brenton have all started their careers at the Court. Many others, including Caryl Churchill, Mark Ravenhill and Sarah Kane have followed. More recently, the theatre has found and fostered new writers such as Polly Stenham, Mike Bartlett, Bola Agbaje, Nick Payne and Rachel De-lahay and produced many iconic plays from Laura Wade's *Posh* to Bruce Norris' *Clybourne Park* and Jez Butterworth's *Jerusalem*. Royal Court plays from every decade are now performed on stage and taught in classrooms across the globe.

Supported by
**ARTS COUNCIL
ENGLAND**

ROYAL COURT SUPPORTERS

The Royal Court has significant and longstanding relationships with many organisations and individuals who provide vital support. It is this support that makes possible its unique playwriting and audience development programmes.

Coutts supports Innovation at the Royal Court. The Genesis Foundation supports the Royal Court's work with International Playwrights. Theatre Local is sponsored by Bloomberg. AlixPartners support The Big Idea at the Royal Court. The Jerwood Charitable Foundation supports emerging writers through the Jerwood New Playwrights series. The Andrew Lloyd Webber Foundation supports the Royal Court's Studio, which aims to seek out, nurture and support emerging playwrights. The Pinter Commission is given annually by his widow, Lady Antonia Fraser, to support a new commission at the Royal Court.

PUBLIC FUNDING
Arts Council England, London
British Council

CHARITABLE DONATIONS
Martin Bowley Charitable Trust

Cowley Charitable Trust
The Dorset Foundation
The Eranda Foundation
Genesis Foundation
The Golden Bottle Trust
The Haberdashers' Company
The Idlewild Trust
Jerwood Charitable Foundation
Marina Kleinwort Trust
The Andrew Lloyd Webber Foundation
John Lyon's Charity
Clare McIntyre's Bursary
The Andrew W. Mellon Foundation
The David & Elaine Potter Foundation
Rose Foundation
Royal Victoria Hall Foundation
The Sackler Trust
The Sobell Foundation
John Thaw Foundation
The Vandervell Foundation
Sir Siegmund Warburg's Voluntary Settlement
The Garfield Weston Foundation
The Wolfson Foundation

CORPORATE SUPPORTERS & SPONSORS
AKA
Alix Partners
American Airlines
Aqua Financial Solutions Ltd
BBC
Bloomberg

Café Colbert
Coutts
Fever-Tree
Gedye & Sons
Kudos Film & Television
MAC
Moët & Chandon
Quintessentially Vodka
Smythson of Bond Street
White Light Ltd

BUSINESS ASSOCIATES, MEMBERS & BENEFACTORS
Annoushka
Auerbach & Steele Opticians
Bank of America Merrill Lynch
Byfield Consultancy
Capital MSL
Cream
Lazard
Vanity Fair
Waterman Group

DEVELOPMENT ADVOCATES
Elizabeth Bandeen
Anthony Burton CBE
Piers Butler
Sindy Caplan
Sarah Chappatte
Cas Donald (Vice Chair)
Celeste Fenichel
Piers Gibson
Emma Marsh (Chair)
Deborah Shaw Marquardt (Vice Chair)
Tom Siebens
Sian Westerman
Daniel Winterfeldt

Supported by
ARTS COUNCIL ENGLAND

Innovation Partner

INDIVIDUAL MEMBERS

MAJOR DONORS

Anonymous
Eric Abraham
Ray Barrell & Ursula Van Almsick
Rob & Siri Cope
Cas Donald
Lydia & Manfred Gorvy
Richard & Marcia Grand
Jack & Linda Keenan
Adam Kenwright
Mandeep Manku
Miles Morland
Mr & Mrs Sandy Orr
NoraLee & Jon Sedmak
Deborah Shaw &
Stephen Marquardt
Jan & Michael Topham
Monica B Voldstad

MOVER-SHAKERS

Anonymous
Christine Collins
Jordan Cook
Mr & Mrs Roderick Jack
Duncan Matthews QC
Mr & Mrs Timothy D Proctor
Ian & Carol Sellars

BOUNDARY-BREAKERS

Anonymous
Katie Bradford
Piers & Melanie Gibson
David Harding
Madeleine Hodgkin
Nicola Kerr
Philip & Joan Kingsley
Emma Marsh
Clive & Sally Sherling
Edgar & Judith Wallner
Mr & Mrs Nick Wheeler

GROUND-BREAKERS

Anonymous
Allen Appen & Jane Wiest
Moira Andreae
Mr & Mrs Simon Andrews
Nick Archdale
Charlotte Asprey
Jane Attias
Elizabeth & Adam Bandeen
Michael Bennett
Sam & Rosie Berwick
Dr Kate Best
Christopher Bevan
Sarah & David Blomfield
Deborah Brett

Mr & Mrs William Broeksmit
Peter & Romey Brown
Joanna Buckenham
Lois Moore & Nigel Burridge
Clive & Helena Butler
Piers Butler
Sindy & Jonathan Caplan
Gavin & Lesley Casey
Sarah & Philippe Chappatte
Tim & Caroline Clark
Carole & Neville Conrad
Andrea & Anthony Coombs
Clyde Cooper
Ian & Caroline Cormack
Mr & Mrs Cross
Andrew & Amanda Cryer
Alison Davies
Roger & Alison De Haan
Matthew Dean
Polly Devlin OBE
Rob & Cherry Dickins
Robyn Durie
Glenn & Phyllida Earle
Graham & Susanna Edwards
The Edwin Fox Foundation
Lisa Erikson & Edward Ocampo
Mark & Sarah Evans
Celeste & Peter Fenichel
Margy Fenwick
Beverley Gee
Nick & Julie Gould
Lord & Lady Grabiner
Jill Hackel & Andrzej Zarzycki
Carol Hall
Stephen & Jennifer Harper
Mr & Mrs Sam Haubold
Gordon & Brette Holmes
Kate Hudspeth
Damien Hyland
Suzie & David Hyman
Amanda & Chris Jennings
Melanie J Johnson
Nicholas Jones
Dr Evi Kaplanis
Susanne Kapoor
David P Kaskel & Christopher A Teano
Vincent & Amanda Keaveny
Peter & Maria Kellner
Dominic Kendrick
Steve Kingshott

Mr & Mrs Pawel Kisielewski
Mr & Mrs David & Sarah Kowitz
Rosemary Leith
Daisy & Richard Littler
Kathryn Ludlow
Beatrice & James Lupton CBE
Suzanne Mackie
Dr Ekaterina Malievskaia & George Goldsmith
Christopher Marek Rencki
Mr & Mrs Marsden
Mrs Janet Martin
Andrew McIver
Barbara Minto
Takehito Mitsui
Angelie Moledina
Riley Morris
Peter & Maggie Murray-Smith
Ann & Gavin Neath CBE
Clive & Annie Norton
Jonathan Och & Rita Halbright
Georgia Oetker
James Orme-Smith
Sir William & Lady Vanessa Patey
Andrea & Hilary Ponti
Annie & Preben Prebensen
Wendy & Philip Press
Paul & Gill Robinson
Andrew & Ariana Rodger
Daniel Romualdez
Corinne Rooney
Sir & Lady Ruddock
William & Hilary Russell
Sally & Anthony Salz
Bhags Sharma
The Michael & Melanie Sherwood Charitable Foundation
Tom Siebens & Mimi Parsons
Andy Simpkin
Anthony Simpson & Susan Boster
Andrea Sinclair & Serge Kremer
Paul & Rita Skinner
Brian Smith
Saadi & Zeina Soudavar
Sue St Johns
The Ulrich Family
Amanda Vail

Constanze Von Unruh
Ian & Victoria Watson & The Watson Foundation
Jens Smith Wergeland
Matthew & Sian Westerman
Mrs Alexandra Whiley
Anne-Marie Williams
Sir Robert & Lady Wilson
Mr Daniel Winterfeldt & Mr Jonathan Leonhart
Katherine & Michael Yates

With thanks to our Friends, Stage-Taker and Ice-Breaker members whose support we greatly appreciate.

Make a Donation

By making a donation to the Royal Court you can help us to respond to new and established playwrights, and supply them with the time, resources and environment to follow their imagination and exceed their potential.

Help us to make the Royal Court the renowned international success that it is.

To make a donation to the Royal Court, please:
Call Anna Sampson on 020 7565 5049
Email annasampson@royalcourttheatre.com
Visit royalcourttheatre.com/support-us/make-a-donation

Thank you in advance for supporting our work and changing theatre forever.

www.royalcourttheatre.com

The English Stage Company at the Royal Court Theatre is a registered charity (No. 231242).

Photo: John Haynes

KHANDAN

Gurpreet Kaur Bhatti

KHANDAN

OBERON BOOKS
LONDON

WWW.OBERONBOOKS.COM

First published in 2014 by Oberon Books Ltd
521 Caledonian Road, London N7 9RH
Tel: +44 [0] 20 7607 3637 / Fax: +44 [0] 20 7607 3629
e-mail: info@oberonbooks.com
www.oberonbooks.com

A catalogue record for this book is available from the British Library.

PB ISBN: 978-1-78319-093-5
E ISBN: 978-1-78319-592-3

Cover image: Ujjal Didar Singh

Printed, bound and converted
by CPI Group [UK] Ltd, Croydon, CR0 4YY.

Visit www.oberonbooks.com to read more about all our books and to buy them. You will also find features, author interviews and news of any author events, and you can sign up for e-newsletters so that you're always first to hear about our new releases.

For Amal, Uma, Gurpal, Amanneet, Harneet and Harry

Characters

JEETO GILL
60s, a portly, kind looking, forceful widow with
dangerous eyes, mother of PAL and COOKIE

LIZ GILL
early 30s, white, loud, big hearted and exuding
cheap glamour, wife of PAL

PAL GILL
early 30s, powerfully built leonine alpha male,
ridden with ambition

COOKIE SAMRA
early 40s, ferocious, rough, successful, sister to
PAL, married to MAJOR

MAJOR SAMRA
mid 40s, overweight, greying, quiet, nervy,
husband to COOKIE

REEMA GILL
late 20s, elegant, serious, rejected wife of JITI –
PAL and COOKIE's cousin in India

Location
Suburb of a city

Setting
The Gill family living room

ACT ONE

SCENE ONE

A few weeks before Christmas. A large bright nouveau riche living room space in neutral colours opens out into a modern well-equipped country style kitchen fitted with a breakfast bar. The atmosphere is regal, comfortable, vast, blank. Huge stainless steel pans sit on the hob. A mahogany sideboard, dining table and chairs occupy part of the living room area and a DFS leather extendable armchair is plonked in the middle. Small, decorative tables are scattered around. Family photographs in gold frames adorn the walls alongside images of the Golden Temple and assorted Sikh Gurus. There is a plush burgundy carpet and a large plasma screen in one corner.

JEETO, 60s, a portly, kind-looking woman with dangerous eyes walks into her home. She wears a bright blue tabard on top of an old flowery shalwar kameez. Carrying a leather handbag over her shoulder, she absent-mindedly holds a wad of letters which she has just picked up. JEETO sings/hums 'Challa', a famous Punjabi folk song, this morphs into the 'Oh na na na' chorus from Rihanna's 'What's My Name'. She goes to the kitchen and calls.

JEETO: *(Shouts.)* Pal!

> *Fills a pan with cold water.*

> *(Shouts.)* Chah peeneeyeh? *[Do you want a cup of tea?]*

> *Puts the pan on the hob. Chucks a couple of teabags, green cardamom, black cardamom and a cinnamon stick into the pan.*

> *(Shouts.)* Pal!

> *She takes off her tabard and goes to seat her significant bottom on the DFS chair. Puts the post down on a small table next to her. She reaches for her bag and takes out a framed black and white photograph of a handsome, distinguished male. She looks at it with long hard love. Then puts it on the table next to her. Stares at it.*

JEETO: *(To the photo.)* Chah peeneeyeh? *[Do you want a cup of tea?] (A beat.)* Only joking. Stupid. Stupid man.

LIZ, 30s, white, loud, big hearted and exuding cheap glamour breezes in. She's wearing fashionable too tight clothes and struggles with a load of shopping bags and an advent calendar. She puts everything on the floor and addresses JEETO as she admires the calendar.

LIZ: The kids made me an advent calendar out of toilet rolls and cornflakes packets. Nice innit? They stuck a smartie with sellotape in all the windows. *(Thinks/A beat.)* You lot'll have to have 'em.

She heads out.

JEETO: Nee Koorih! *[Hey you girl!]*

LIZ stops, sighs, covers her head with a scarf and goes over to touch JEETO's feet [in the way a Punjabi daughter-in-law would touch her mother-in-law's feet].

JEETO: Chah!

LIZ: In a minute.

LIZ nips back out. JEETO picks up the photo, looks longingly at it again. Puts it back in the bag. LIZ returns holding a few more supermarket carriers.

JEETO: And put plenty milk. You never put enough milk.

LIZ: Cos it's dairy innit.

JEETO: Oh choop khar. *[Be quiet].*

LIZ: I'm not supposed to have dairy. Remember? Stops the egg sticking to the womb lining.

JEETO: Kee ponkee jundiah? *[What's she going on about?]*

LIZ: Or something.

LIZ opens a packet of fancy biscuits and considers them.

LIZ: Boasters were on special offer. *(Takes one.)* One boaster never killed anyone did it? *(She eats.)*

JEETO: Eat kurreeh eat. You need more flesh on that white body of yours. Do you want my grandson to break your bones when he comes out of you?

LIZ: You have the rest *(Passes biscuits to JEETO.).*

JEETO: Don't worry they can fix bones these days. Not like back home, when my Nanaji broke his toe, the doctors amputated his foot. You are lucky that won't happen to you.

LIZ starts putting the shopping away.

JEETO: Pal?

LIZ: Cash and Carry.

JEETO: Stock should be there from the morning.

LIZ: He was too busy in the morning.

JEETO: Busy? What is this busy? These days everyone is always moaning, groaning they are bastard busy. You have to find time if you are running a business. Pal's daddy would have been to the Cash and Carry before Pal and Cookie put on school uniforms.

LIZ puts the shopping away. JEETO takes her shoes and socks off.

JEETO: Chillumchee *[Basin].*

LIZ fills a basin with water and squeezes some soap into it.

LIZ: I gooned the atta *[kneaded the dough]* before I went to work.

JEETO: I'll make the rotis.

LIZ brings the basin over, JEETO rolls up her shalwar.

LIZ: I'll make 'em, yours are too fat.

JEETO points to the calendar and puts her feet to soak in the basin.

JEETO: Show me.

LIZ takes it to her. JEETO has a good look.

JEETO: Very colourful.

LIZ goes to get a load of toddlers' pictures. JEETO opens a day on the calendar and eats a smartie.

LIZ: The parents don't want these ones. They say they run out of wall space. Say after a while they all look the same.

JEETO: I like this one with the sheep.

9

LIZ: That's supposed to be me.

JEETO hands the pictures back. LIZ contemplates them.

LIZ: You know if your grandson or granddaughter does come, I'll never leave him. You know like at nursery.

LIZ pours milk and half a bag of sugar into the pan. Turns the hob off. Pours two cups of tea out.

JEETO: You won't need to, while he is small I am here.

LIZ: Oh yeah…course.

LIZ hands her a cup of tea. JEETO looks down at the cup.

JEETO: Next time put more milk.

LIZ: One small cup can't hurt. *(She drinks.)*

JEETO: You girls these days have it easy. If I'd given my mother-in-law tea like this, she would have beaten me with an iron bar. And if my mother-in-law had given her mother-in-law tea like this, her mother-in-law would have poisoned her.

LIZ takes the Advent calendar from JEETO.

LIZ: *(Tuts annoyed.)* You've eaten Christmas Eve!

JEETO: Oh choop kar *[be quiet]*. What is this Christmas anyway? Everyone just spending more and more bastard pesah *[money]*.

LIZ: It's not just money, it's for the kids innit? And for everyone to have fun with their families.

JEETO: Fun?

LIZ: There's more to life than the shop Mum.

JEETO: We always stay open on Christmas Day. The only shop in town. Customers come from miles.

LIZ: Pal's…closing this year.

JEETO: Closing?

LIZ: That's what he said.

JEETO: Acha. We will see. You people shouldn't be afraid of hard work.

LIZ: He's not.

JEETO: Shop work is hard but it's better than cleaning toilets. Did you know I cleaned toilets when I first came to this country?

LIZ: You mention it most days.

JEETO: When Pal's father got the keys to the shop, he took my hand and he said.

LIZ and JEETO: Jeeto, you'll never clean after another gorah *[white man]* again…

LIZ: Come on Mum, you must have to do some cleaning in the hospital.

JEETO: Wiping the tea trolley is different from putting my hand where *[white]* goreh bottoms have been.

She reaches for the post and hands it to LIZ who starts going through it.

LIZ: My phone bill, your phone bill, Pal's phone bill. Electric. This one's for you.

She hands JEETO a blue airmail letter. JEETO studies it.

LIZ: Who's it from?

LIZ grabs another Boaster. Hops onto the Breakfast Bar where she perches cross-legged.

JEETO: Chacha.

LIZ: Oh right. Hang on, hang on a minute, I know this one… that's Pal's dad's older brother.

JEETO: Younger brother stupid!

LIZ: I hope no one's died.

JEETO: No one back home left to die. Chacha needs money. Like the rest of this bastard world.

LIZ holds up another child's picture.

LIZ: This one's the Virgin Mary, holding baby Jesus.

JEETO: You think your Mary was a virgin?

LIZ: Maybe.

JEETO: Is this why I have no grandson? What is wrong with you people? Uncross your legs Kurreeh!

Suddenly all the lights go out. JEETO and LIZ gasp. A glow stick becomes visible, it spells out I LUV U in LIZ's direction.

LIZ: *(Screeches with joy.)* Ah, that is wicked!

PAL, mid 30s, turns the lights on as LIZ giggles with glee. He's a powerfully built leonine alpha male. Buoyant, lively and slightly drunk, he wears a high street suit.

PAL: Harj had a box left over from fireworks, he was selling 'em in the pub.

JEETO: You had a box left over from fireworks in the shop.

PAL: Can't I buy my wife a present now?

LIZ: Course you can babes.

JEETO: Fer Pub gaya? *[So you went to the pub?]*

LIZ gets PAL a cup of tea.

PAL: Satwant's birthday, I had to go for one.

LIZ: Don't say you did karaoke.

PAL: I had to.

LIZ: Without me? Pal!

PAL: It was his birthday.

LIZ: Let's do it now. Go on you and me.

PAL: Not now.

JEETO: Cash and Carry nee gaya?

PAL: I'll go in the morning.

LIZ: Go on.

PAL: I haven't had me chah!

LIZ: Pal!

PAL sighs, plonks down his tea and wearily slicks back his hair. He sings reluctantly while LIZ does the 'Oh oh ohs' between each line.

PAL: *(Sings.)* When you smile the world is brighter. You touch my hand and I'm a king. *(Touches LIZ's hand.)* Your kiss to me is worth a fortune. Your love for me is everything. I guess I'll never know the reason why you love me like you do.

LIZ joins in the chorus. They do the affected Elvis mannerisms and sing well and in tune.

BOTH: That's the wonder…the wonder of you… Ooooh… ooohh…

They kiss.

JEETO: Is any cunjar *[whore]* ever going to hoover this carpet?

LIZ: I did it yesterday.

LIZ starts making rotis. PAL loosens his tie and takes off his shirt. He finds a casual top hanging off a door and puts it on.

JEETO: *(Pointing at the carpet.)* This colour shows every crumb and fluff. If you got the patterned one like I said you would only need to hoover once a month.

PAL: I keep saying get a cleaner.

JEETO: And throw more peseh down the toilet?

PAL: It's not that expensive.

JEETO: I don't want some kurreeh *[girl]* looking through my bin, telling the world how many times I blow my nose.

LIZ opens a shopping bag.

LIZ: There were loads of offers in Asda. What do you think of this for Cookie?

She holds up a sparkly top.

PAL: Alright.

She produces a man's jumper.

LIZ: I know this is a bit…boring but Major'll like it. I mean he'll wear it.

JEETO: Have you got figures for November?

PAL: Not yet.

LIZ: The girls want Ann Summers vouchers…

PAL: But Simmy's only eleven.

LIZ: I told her Cookie'll go mad. Anyway I've got them a couple of DVDs and sparkly hair bobbles.

JEETO: Mark my words, figures for November will be down.

PAL: They won't be. And if they are, I'll make it up in December.

JEETO: Daddy always opened Christmas Day.

PAL: Yeah, well, it's up to me now.

JEETO: You should listen to people who have the experience. If you stay open you increase profits. Work hard and one day you might even open another shop. Daddy always dreamed of you having your own business.

PAL: And I will, just might not be a shop.

JEETO: Kee? *[What?]*

LIZ: Pal's working on a new idea Mum. You should hear it.

JEETO: Cookie had a good November.

PAL: You get tips in a salon.

JEETO picks up her letter. PAL observes her.

PAL: Chacha?

JEETO nods.

PAL: *(To JEETO.)* How much is he asking for this time?

JEETO: Chacha is looking after your land.

PAL: I've told you I don't want it.

JEETO: And the kauthee *[house]* for when I retire. He's building me my own bathroom remember?

PAL: You've got an ensuite upstairs!

JEETO: Did I mention he is painting the verandah? In a few years I will be sitting outside on the old munjah. Breathing in the smell of fresh saag and mackee dhi roti cooking on the choolah. Watching the Pappar man go past on his bicycle while I read letters from my grandson.

LIZ: He'll probably Skype you.

JEETO: Stupid! You think there are computers in the pind [village]?

PAL: Mum! India's the technology centre of the world. With the amount of money we send him, Chacha could open an Apple Store in the pind.

JEETO: Hah, hah, hah [yes, yes, yes], you know everything. (Opens letter.)

PAL: What's the point anyway? You're not going.

JEETO: (Reads.) Dear Bhanji, Every time I pick up the phone, tears flow from my eyes. So I am writing you this letter, bearing a terrible pain, one which only a parent can understand.

PAL and LIZ gather round.

JEETO: (Reading.) I told you many times that my son was mixing with a wrong crowd. And now, Jiti has left the kauthee [house] for good. He said he doesn't want to be a farmer any more. He said he wants to be a hero in Bollywood.

PAL: He'll be back in a few days.

JEETO: (Reads.) I have repaid all his debts, but his bad history in this area means the men will not let him enter the village, ever again. Reema is here with me and is a great comfort. Still, everyone is blaming the poor girl. They say she should have looked after her husband better. The neighbours are calling her names, they say they always knew she was bad news.

LIZ: Why?

JEETO: She's from Jullundhar. (Reads.) I beg you Bhanji, please send her a ticket to come to UK.

PAL: What?

JEETO: (Reads.) My daughter-in-law has no future here in Punjab. And you must realise for everyone's sake, it is best that she leaves. Reema is a good girl Bhanji, she is

15

more my child than my son ever was. I beg you, show pity on her and give her this chance. Yours most respectfully, Jasdev Singh Gill.

She puts the letter down, looks at PAL.

PAL: No…no way… If she leaves the pind, who's gonna make Chacha's roti? Who'll wash his kachees *[underwear]* and cut his toenails?

JEETO: We have three empty bedrooms.

LIZ: It's not easy being a daughter-in-law.

PAL: Mum!

JEETO: Kee? *[What?]*

PAL: Did you know about this?

JEETO: How could I know?

PAL: She can't just turn up here.

JEETO: That girl is our responsibility.

PAL: And what happens after she arrives? I'm the one who'll have to buy her a bus pass, teach her how to use a till, take her up Primark…

LIZ: Maybe she can come for a bit.

PAL and JEETO eye one another gravely.

PAL: She's not planning a city break Liz.

JEETO: Your Chacha is old. It's not safe for a woman without her husband on that farm. If you don't care what happens to her, at least care about our honour.

PAL: She's Jiti's wife, he should be looking after her.

JEETO: You think we should leave her to rot in that house? Watching your Chacha cry into his lassi?

PAL: We can't afford it.

JEETO: If you open Christmas Day you could pay for a ticket.

LIZ: Come and have your roti.

PAL goes to sit at the table. LIZ presents him with a range of dishes and a pile of chapattis. He eats hungrily.

JEETO: Cookie is opening Christmas Eve till 9 p.m.

PAL: Perhaps Cookie can buy a ticket then.

LIZ brings JEETO her food on a tray.

LIZ: You'll have to put the tree up soon Pal. I'll ask if the girls want to come over and help.

JEETO: Daddy would have done it already.

PAL pushes his plate away, half slams the table. Gets up.

PAL: Oh yeah. He'd have stuck some ragged old tinsel on that wonky silver tree we've had since 1985.

JEETO stands up, her feet are still in the basin.

JEETO: You show your daddy some respect!

PAL opens the fridge, gets a beer, holds it up.

PAL: This is what Daddy respected.

He puts the beer down hard on the table.

JEETO: Cookie walked before she was one years old. Do you know that? She would cry because her feet felt cold on the lino in that stinking kamarah *[room]* we shared with Uncle Nagra. We lived on roti *[bread]* and dayhee *[yoghurt]* for a month because Daddy wanted his daughter to feel carpet under her feet. And when we brought you back from the hospital he held you up in that stinking kamarah and smiled and he said 'This is your country son. You show those haramzadeh *[bastards]* who call me Paki and spit at my back. You show them!'

PAL takes a swig of the beer and goes back to his food.

JEETO: He did everything for you children. And you cannot help your chacha.

JEETO sits down. LIZ starts clearing up.

PAL: You expect me to provide for her, just like that?

LIZ gets a text.

LIZ: Cookie hasn't cooked so they're coming over.

She gets her coat.

LIZ: I'll need more butter to chopurr the rotis. *(To PAL.)* Have you got any change?

JEETO: Biscuit jar.

LIZ takes a large glass jar out of a cupboard. It's full of cash. She takes some money and heads out. JEETO puts her food to one side. Starts drying her feet.

PAL: How are your feet?

JEETO: Swollen.

PAL: I want you to pack the hospital in.

JEETO: These hands need to work. *(Eyes PAL.)* Daddy promised Chacha he would look after him. You have to be Daddy now.

PAL: I'm doing my best.

JEETO: I want that girl here.

PAL: *(A beat.)* We'll see.

PAL picks up the beer, opens it, takes a swig. Mariah Carey's 'All I want for Christmas' plays into the next scene.

SCENE TWO

New Year's Eve. The same living room is lavishly adorned with Christmas decorations, crammed full with cards and a lit up B&Q tree looms at the back. COOKIE SAMRA, early 40s, ferocious, rough, hard-faced and immaculately made up, sits at the table, texting avidly on her iPhone. COOKIE drips with gold, and wears an expensive, ultra fashionable shalwar kameez. She puts the phone down, wanders over to the kitchen area, opens the fridge, stares into it. She has a quick look around and carefully removes a bottle of white wine. COOKIE hurriedly unscrews it, takes a long swig and puts it back.

COOKIE walks back to the table, opens her designer handbag, takes out Gold Spot mouth freshener, sprays it into her mouth and retouches her lipstick. Her phone rings, she scans the caller's name, takes a deep breath, sits back on the dining chair, answers the phone, talks quietly.

COOKIE: At my mum's… They're picking up my cousin's wife from the airport…I dunno, might be five minutes, might be five hours, you know what they're like… I can't can I?… I'm sorry…

Person on the other end puts the phone down. COOKIE chucks her phone down onto the table. Seconds later it rings again.

COOKIE: What d'you do that for?… I can't can I? We're all supposed to be going to this party at Inderjit's house… No…I told you…

LIZ enters, she's glammed up too in a shalwar kameez, but carries a broom and cleaning materials. COOKIE's getting angrier.

COOKIE: I said… What?… Fuck off then!

She suddenly notices LIZ staring at her. Composes herself.

COOKIE: *(Into phone.)* I mean…er…I'm sorry…the salon's closed until the second of January. If you ring back then, you can make an appointment.

She turns her phone off. Eyes LIZ uneasily.

COOKIE: One of my regulars…she…er…wants…her… moustache waxed for this evening.

LIZ: Bit late now innit?

COOKIE: That's what I said. I mean I can't drop everything, just cos she's got a bit of regrowth.

LIZ starts sweeping the floor.

LIZ: New Year's Eve innit, everyone wants to look their best.

COOKIE: What you doing?

LIZ: Making it nice for her when she arrives. So she feels comfortable.

COOKIE: She's gonna be living for free in a five bedroom house, you don't get more comfortable than that.

LIZ: Might be hard for her, getting used to the pace of life y'know.

COOKIE: Stick some Indian films on for her. That'll keep her happy. Oh and get some cream cakes, they like cream cakes for some reason. If there's any in the shop past the sell-by date she can have them. *(Fiddles with her phone.)* Thought they'd be back by now.

LIZ: Mum says she'll be helping round the house when I'm at work and when the little one comes along.

COOKIE: Have you got some news?

LIZ: Not this month.

COOKIE: I wouldn't worry about it. You're not missing much.

COOKIE checks her Rolex. She's getting annoyed.

COOKIE: Where are they? I can't be dealing with this Indian timing.

LIZ: Traffic innit.

COOKIE: Suppose she'll wanna go sightseeing at the weekend. Buckingham Palace and all that shit.

LIZ: Dunno.

COOKIE: They all wanna go there. And Madame Tussauds. Five quid for a diet coke it was when that Jiti came. I can't be dealing with it. I told Mum I'm not taking her. You lot'll have to do it.

LIZ: I don't mind.

COOKIE: Suppose Major could go.

LIZ: So you closed tomorrow?

COOKIE: Yeah. You can't do a Brazilian with a hangover. Couple of girls are going round to clients' houses.

LIZ: You could do with a day off. Be nice for Simmy and Jasmin.

COOKIE: They're not bothered.

LIZ: Thought they'd be coming to Inderjit's.

COOKIE: No, they're going round some schoolfriend's. Major's dropping them.

Sound of front door opening outside.

COOKIE: At last. What's her name again?

LIZ: Reema.

MAJOR enters. He's mid-40s, overweight, greying, badly dressed in an ill-fitting suit, quiet, nervy.

LIZ: Alright Major.

MAJOR: Alright.

He takes off his jacket to reveal a bright shirt patterned with aeroplanes.

COOKIE tuts in shock.

COOKIE: What the hell are you wearing?

MAJOR: What's wrong?

COOKIE: Looks like one of them crimplene shirt sets you got for our wedding.

LIZ: Do you want chah?

MAJOR: Yeah, go on.

LIZ puts the tea on.

COOKIE: You're supposed to wear that Paul Smith one I bought you for Christmas.

MAJOR: I thought this was it.

COOKIE: I left it on the bed. *(Tuts.)* You have to embarrass me don't you?

MAJOR: Nobody cares what I'm wearing.

COOKIE: Course they do. You know what Inderjit and them lot are like. They'll be laughing their heads off, saying we can't afford designer.

MAJOR: They won't.

COOKIE: Why not just get one off that eBay and kill me now? You'll have to go home and change.

MAJOR: I'm not going home.

COOKIE: You are.

MAJOR: Liz is making chah now.

COOKIE: You're going home.

He comes to sit down. Checks his watch. LIZ gives him his tea.

MAJOR: They still not back?

LIZ: Maybe the plane was late.

COOKIE: He could have texted, I could have gone to meet Tracey and them lot. They were going up TGIs for cocktails. *(Tuts.)* Bloody Indian Timing.

LIZ: *(To MAJOR.)* Are the girls excited about New Year's Eve?

MAJOR: *(Beams.)* Oh yeah. There's a load of them round Nina's house having a sleepover. They're all in their pyjamas and they're gonna watch that new Disney film…

COOKIE: So they say.

MAJOR: They've got about ten boxes of Krispy Kremes. And Nina's mum's making them hot chocolate with marshmallows.

COOKIE: They'll probably do drugs later.

MAJOR: What d'you have to say that for?

COOKIE: They're teenagers innit. That's what they do.

LIZ: Not Simmy and Jasmin.

MAJOR: You're bad-minded you are.

COOKIE: I'm joking! I don't want either of them turning into a smackhead do I? Like some sullah.

MAJOR: Do you have to use that word?

COOKIE: Who are you? Ofsted or something? I'm only having a laugh. It's New Year's Eve innit.

MAJOR walks round to get more tea. COOKIE eyes his shirt, makes a face.

COOKIE: You look like Thomas the tank engine.

MAJOR: They're aeroplanes not trains!

LIZ: Shall I get you one of Pal's? He won't mind.

MAJOR: Go on then.

LIZ exits. Silence. COOKIE's phone pings as she receives another text.

MAJOR: Who's that?

COOKIE: Tracey. Letting me know what time they're meeting.

MAJOR: Thought you told her you can't make it.

COOKIE: She's just letting me know.

They contemplate one another awkwardly.

MAJOR: Let's try and have a nice time tonight.

COOKIE: Okay.

LIZ comes back holding an aubergine designer shirt. MAJOR puts it on. They watch him, it's ridiculously tight.

LIZ: Er…how is it?

MAJOR: *(Optimistic.)* Alright, yeah. Bit tight under the arms.

COOKIE: What do you expect? *(To LIZ.)* Do you know what he eats for lunch?

MAJOR: Don't start!

COOKIE: Domino's on Monday. McDonald's on Tuesday and Wednesday.

MAJOR: Only the filet of fish.

COOKIE: With fries and milkshake! Then Nando's on Thursday.

MAJOR: Not every Thursday.

COOKIE: Then Domino's again on Friday.

MAJOR: I don't have any breakfast. I never have breakfast.

COOKIE: It's a wonder he can walk to the car.

Sound of the front door opening. LIZ jumps up.

LIZ: They're here!

COOKIE and MAJOR turn to face the entrance. PAL, JEETO and REEMA walk in. REEMA is elegant, serious-looking and dressed in a tasteful shalwar kameez and shawl.

JEETO: Reema, this is Cookie.

REEMA: Hello Bhanji.

COOKIE: Call me Cookie.

JEETO: And Major.

MAJOR: *(Hands together.)* Helloji.

REEMA: Hello.

PAL: This is Liz, my wife.

LIZ: Sat siri akal.

REEMA: Hello.

JEETO: Sit.

She indicates the armchair to REEMA who sits down. LIZ starts making tea.

JEETO: *(To REEMA.)* Chah peeneeyeh?

REEMA: Just a glass of water please.

LIZ: You must need chah, it's freezing out!

REEMA: I'm fine really.

LIZ gets her a glass of water.

JEETO: Meh pushaab karkihoneehyeh. *[I'm just going for a wee.]*

She exits. PAL notices MAJOR's shirt, his face falls.

PAL: What you wearing that for?

MAJOR: Liz said you wouldn't mind.

PAL: Brand new that is. I got it for tonight.

MAJOR: I was just trying it on.

PAL: And you've ripped it!

MAJOR: Only the seam, no one'll notice!

He starts taking it off.

PAL: Leave it! I can't wear it now can I?

They compose themselves and all turn to smile awkwardly at REEMA.

COOKIE: So…er…how's Chacha?

REEMA: He's…coping.

COOKIE: He's proper nice isn't he? I went back to the pind *[village]* when I was a kid and he taught me how to milk the mudge.

REEMA: That's nice.

COOKIE: Yeah. So…er…how is the mudge?

REEMA: Papaji doesn't keep buffaloes any more.

COOKIE: That's a shame. Oh he made sure we had a right good time. I remember he took me and Daddy up Chaura Bazaar and I managed to get a whole Golguppa in my mouth, in one go. Massive it was. Jiti was well impressed.

Awkward silence.

MAJOR: Has…er…Jiti been in touch?

REEMA: No.

Awkward silence. REEMA opens her bag, takes a few items out – book, purse, papers, she puts them on a side table.

COOKIE: Probably busy isn't he? I mean everyone's rushed off their feet in Bollywood.

REEMA: I have some presents for you. Bhanji, Liz.

She hands COOKIE and LIZ each a small wrapped package. They open them to reveal small carved animals.

LIZ: I've always wanted an elephant!

COOKIE: Mine stinks!

REEMA: They're hand carved. From Sandalwood.

LIZ: Ah, they're lovely. You shouldn't have!

COOKIE: *(Sniffs.)* Smells like that Britney Spears' Fantasy.

MAJOR: *(To REEMA.)* Flight teekseeh? *[How was the flight?]*

REEMA: Fine.

LIZ: I've made dhal and bhindi, when you're ready.

REEMA: Actually I had dinner on the plane.

LIZ: Oh. So what do you think of it so far? You know, England?

REEMA: Well, it's very dark outside…

LIZ: Course. Er…do you like the street lamps?

REEMA: *(Nods.)* Er…yes… You have a very beautiful house.

JEETO returns.

JEETO: Come Reema, I'll show you your room. Liz bring my chah. *(To PAL.)* Suitcase.

PAL: Major'll get it.

He chucks his car keys to MAJOR who catches them, sighs and follows REEMA and JEETO out. LIZ makes JEETO's tea.

LIZ: Very refined isn't she? Proper sophisticated.

COOKIE: She's a teacher innit. Probably speaks better English than you.

PAL: And you.

LIZ: You'll never guess what Pal. Some woman just rang Cookie up asking her to wax her moustache tonight.

PAL: Bit late innit.

LIZ exits with the tea. PAL beholds his sister's upper lip. COOKIE is texting.

PAL: You wanna do your own, it's growing back.

COOKIE: Shut up.

COOKIE gets another text.

PAL: *(Indicating the phone.)* Better not be that fucking Tariq.

COOKIE: It's my mate Tracey.

PAL: Is that what you call him nowadays?

COOKIE: Get lost.

PAL: You got no sharam, you know that?

COOKIE: You're the one who married the goreeh.

PAL: She makes better roti than you, and she hasn't got a tache. Anyway least I had the guts to come clean.

COOKIE: You could have come home with an Albanian crack whore, Mum'd still ask how many biscuits you want with your chah.

PAL: You see him though don't you?

COOKIE: Only cos he lives in the area. I don't see him, see him.

PAL starts fiddling with his iPad.

PAL: You still talk to him though?

COOKIE: Why shouldn't I? You talk to the girls you were at school with.

PAL: That's different.

COOKIE observes PAL on his iPad.

COOKIE: When did you get that?

PAL: Christmas present.

COOKIE: From Liz?

PAL: From me.

COOKIE: You're supposed to give to others at Christmas, not yourself.

PAL: Tax deductible. *(Admiring an app.)* Here, look, this App tells me how much money's going through the till. Updates every five minutes!

COOKIE: You wanna spend your time making money, not counting it.

LIZ comes back in. COOKIE looks over PAL's shoulder.

COOKIE: *(Reads.)* Initial specification for Apna Ghar Nursing Home... Oy, you're not sticking Mum in there!

PAL: Course not. Me and Harj are writing a business plan for a new project.

LIZ: There's a lot of money in nursing homes Cookie.

COOKIE: What do you know about business plans?

PAL: Enough.

> *COOKIE's phone rings.*

COOKIE: Hello… Yeah, hang on a minute…

> *She exits. PAL plays with his iPad. LIZ clears up in the kitchen.*

LIZ: You looking forward to Inderjit's?

PAL: Chicken tikka for starters. Roti, dhal, meat and chol after that. Apna Punjab playing while I neck me second bottle of Johnny Walker. Course I am!

LIZ: Perhaps this'll be our year.

PAL: Definitely.

LIZ: And…perhaps it'll happen.

PAL: Yeah, why not?

LIZ: Cos we've been trying for ages. Years.

PAL: One of them things. Tests came back normal.

LIZ: Yeah…

PAL: Just gonna take time.

LIZ: I don't understand why, that's all.

PAL: Keep trying innit.

LIZ: I could find out about that IVF.

> *LIZ stops, turns to him.*

LIZ: Give us more of a chance.

PAL: We don't need all that. Besides we're young, that stuff's for old people, the ones who've given up.

LIZ: No, it's not.

PAL: Things are alright as they are.

LIZ: I could find out. No harm in finding out.

PAL: Supposed to be expensive.

LIZ: Be worth it if it works.

PAL: Now she's here, there'll be a wedding to sort.

LIZ: Cookie might lend us…

PAL: *(Interrupts/Firm.)* No! No way.

LIZ: I could ask my mum and dad.

PAL: They don't want no brown babies going round their house! Come on, we're trying aren't we?

LIZ: If I knew we definitely could…even if it's ages away, then I'd be alright, but it's not knowing when or if…

PAL: Stop worrying!

LIZ: I just wanna be somebody's mum.

PAL: What are you going on about? You're making it worse!

LIZ: I want a baby Pal.

PAL: Me too. I wanna be the same as other blokes. Pushing swings down the park, buying one of them off road three-wheelers, moaning about being knackered and getting old. It's New Year's Eve, come on, let's go and get hammered.

LIZ: Okay, I'm sorry!

He feels bad, pulls her towards him.

PAL: It's gonna happen. I know it.

He kisses her hard and passionately. LIZ withdraws, finishes clearing up. Covers her disappointment. MAJOR enters, he's holding his iPhone and grinning.

MAJOR: *(Reads.)* Happy New Year to the best dad in the world. Saved you a chocolate sprinkles Krispy Kreme. *(Looks up.)* That's my favourite! *(Reads.)* Love you Sim and Jas. *(COOKIE Enters.)* Remember don't pick us up before noon tomorrow and don't call us, we'll call you. DO NOT CALL, exclamation mark. Exclamation mark. Exclamation mark.

LIZ: You've got good girls Major.

MAJOR: Oh yeah. They make all the rubbish life throws at you seem worth it.

JEETO and REEMA enter. LIZ composes herself.

LIZ: *(To REEMA.)* Do you wanna come to the party?

COOKIE: She's not gonna wanna sing 'Auld Lang Syne' after 9 hours on Air India.

REEMA: I'm okay. It would be nice to go out.

PAL: We haven't got time for her to change.

LIZ: Well you look lovely as you are.

REEMA gathers her things.

JEETO: Reema isn't going.

LIZ: Oh.

REEMA's face falls. COOKIE enters.

JEETO: You look tired.

REEMA: But I'd like to…

JEETO: *(Interrupts.)* Sit down.

REEMA stares at JEETO, then sits.

COOKIE: Right then, let's move.

JEETO sits down.

JEETO: I'm staying with Reema. Here.

PAL: What?

COOKIE: What you on about? Everyone'll be waiting for you to do your boliah *[songs]*. They'll wanna to hear that rude one, y'know about the testicles.

JEETO: *(To REEMA.)* You can see Big Ben on the television.

LIZ: Mum, I pressed your suit and everything!

JEETO: And Reema will help me write the cards for Daddy's patth. *(To REEMA.)* At the end of March we always do a khand patth *[religious service]* for their daddy in the house.

REEMA: Our custom is to do only one patth, the year after a loved one dies. Papaji held one at the Gurdwara.

JEETO: We make the langar *[meal]* here ourselves. You will see what customs money can buy.

COOKIE: But Inderjit's hired a chocolate fountain for the front room.

JEETO: I am tired of going to places on my own.

PAL: We're with you.

JEETO: *(Loud.)* Does anyone under this roof remember my husband?

COOKIE: You think you're the only one who misses him?

PAL: Mum, just come willya…

LIZ: All your friends'll be there.

JEETO: Oh yes, pointing their fingers and staring with their pitying eyes. Look at poor Jeeto, buchareeh *[poor thing].* No husband, no grandson, Jeeto, alone with her bad kismet.

PAL: If Daddy didn't care what they say, why do you?

JEETO starts taking off her shoes.

JEETO: Reema will keep me company.

MAJOR starts to head out.

MAJOR: Happy New Year then.

COOKIE and LIZ follow.

LIZ: See you in 2014.

PAL turns to join them.

PAL: Happy New Year. *(Exits.)*

JEETO opens her bag, finds her husband's photo, puts it on the table next to her.

JEETO: You know when I danced with my husband I was the envy of all the ladies round here. Whenever we went to a party, the other ladies would be walking yards behind their men. But Daddy would hold my hand. Everyone would be looking, whispering – 'see what Gill Sahib is doing'? He'd laugh and say what was the point of marrying this beauty if I can't show her off. That man made my heart beat, he turned me into a somebody.

REEMA: *(Eyeing the photo.)* He was very handsome when he was young.

JEETO: Even more handsome when he died.

REEMA: Papaji cried for days after we got the news.

JEETO: We all cried.

REEMA: Poor Papaji, he has lost his brother and his son. And now I am here.

JEETO: Jiti didn't go to Bollywood did he?

REEMA shakes her head.

JEETO: Was he still taking nusheh *[drugs]?*

REEMA: *(Nods.)* Every drug he could lay his hands on. And drinking, all day and all night.

JEETO: Where is he?

REEMA: We don't know. Jiti took my wedding gold with him when he left. And his mother's. He has broken Papaji's heart.

REEMA starts crying to herself.

JEETO: Acha. *[I see.]* (A beat.) Now you and I are women without men.

REEMA continues to cry silently. JEETO eyes her gravely.

JEETO: Stop your crying kurreeh. No time for tears in UK.

REEMA gets up slowly to get herself a glass of water.

REEMA: Thank you Thyji. For bringing me here.

JEETO: Don't ever thank anyone in the family Reema.

REEMA: I promise I won't be a burden.

JEETO: Burden?

REEMA: *(Nervous.)* I have qualifications. Not just in teaching. I studied economics in college. I know I will have to work. And I'll work hard. Doing whatever, I don't care. I'd like to study some more? Not straight away. But one day. When I've saved some money. If that's alright?

JEETO: First, learn to make the chah.

REEMA: Chah?

JEETO: There's a pattheela *[pan]* behind you. And lachees *[cardamoms]* and longh *[cloves]* and tea bags on the second shelf.

REEMA slowly gets the stuff for the tea.

JEETO: You know I was born twice. Once when I came out of my mother. And then when a 747 landed at Heathrow Airport in 1969.

REEMA makes the tea. JEETO eyes her gravely.

JEETO: It will be the same for you.

Dina Carroll's 'Perfect Year' plays and fuses into…

SCENE THREE (MARCH)

…Sikh religious music. The Christmas decorations are gone and the furniture is pushed back.

White sheets cover the floor and the characters sit on them, hands clasped, legs crossed, heads covered, shoes off, backs to the audience. Music fades.

The Ardaas [Sikh prayer] comes through loudly on a speaker. The congregation stand and join in with the chanting. As it ends, they all bend down and put their foreheads to the floor.

They sit back down. A woman, possibly REEMA, enters carrying a pan of parshad [religious sweet food] and hands it out to the characters who accept it gratefully with both hands and then eat it.

A man, possibly MAJOR, gives out kitchen towels to the congregation. After they have eaten and wiped their hands, they stand, clasp hands and gather round the door to watch the holy book [unseen] being carried out of the house.

Music plays again. The men start removing the white sheets. LIZ and COOKIE are in the kitchen area, making chapattis and stirring huge pots of dhal and sabji. JEETO and REEMA fill thalis with the food and REEMA and the men exit to dole out the thalis to the congregation who are spread throughout the house. Trays of tea follow the thalis out. The actions are repeated so there is a sense of the serving of the congregation as is normal following the khand patth [religious service].

Music fades. The women are in the kitchen area washing up. MAJOR enters.

MAJOR: Binder and them lot want more gulab jaman *[Indian sweets]*.

LIZ: But the kids haven't had any yet.

Someone calls MAJOR from outside, he disappears.

JEETO: Give them to Binder.

LIZ: There aren't enough.

MAJOR reappears.

JEETO: Give them.

LIZ puts gulab jaman into a few bowls onto a tray. REEMA enters, goes to help the women.

MAJOR: And I need five more chahs.

COOKIE doles out five cups of tea onto the same tray.

MAJOR: Binder wants to know if she can take some gulab jaman home.

JEETO: Tell her yes.

MAJOR: And she asked for some sabji. I think she's got visitors later.

MAJOR takes the tray out.

JEETO: *(To COOKIE.)* Sabji pah *[put the sabji]*.

COOKIE puts everything into foil containers. The women carry on clearing up the food.

LIZ: What about Mum's wedding ring? Maybe Binder could have it melted down and made into a bangle.

REEMA and COOKIE laugh.

JEETO: Choop kar! In our culture we take care of people.

COOKIE: She means we have to look like we're taking care of them.

LIZ: Even the ones who hate us like Binder?

REEMA: We take care of them the best.

JEETO: Binder is my good friend.

LIZ: She always ignores me. And if she does talk to me, she never calls me by my name. It's just 'Nee Goreeh' *[Oy, white girl!]*

JEETO: Choop kar. The important thing is everyone came for Daddy.

COOKIE: He was never one for khand patths though was he?

JEETO: Your Daddy believed in God.

COOKIE: Course he did. He just didn't believe in the Gurdwara.

LIZ: He would have enjoyed seeing everyone.

COOKIE: For about five minutes. By this time, him and Uncle Hothi would have sneaked off to the pub, lining up the whisky chasers…

JEETO: Is this the day to be talking about the pub?

MAJOR enters.

COOKIE: Well he would have.

MAJOR: Binder's asking if there's any dhal left.

JEETO: *(Angry.)* Does Binder want the chooni off my head?

LIZ: How come she's still here?

JEETO: *(To COOKIE.)* Dhal pah. *[Put the dhal.]*

MAJOR: Her and Inderjit are doing Zumba on the Wii. They're practising figures of eight. *(Demonstrates.)*

PAL enters with his head covered. He carries a couple of empty thalis over to the kitchen area.

PAL: I sorted the giani *[priest].*

COOKIE: How much?

PAL: Twelve hundred.

LIZ: Pal!

REEMA: It's too much. In India nobody bothers with this ShowSha.

PAL: Only cos you're all skint! Gianiji did Daddy's first patth and last year. And today everyone's been saying how beautiful the kirtan was so I reckon he's due a rise. Anyway I can afford it.

COOKIE: *(Mimics.)* Anyway I can afford it. Stop showing off willya!

PAL: Just cos I fancy giving the man a tip…

JEETO: Gianiji is not a waiter at Pizza Hut. That money is going to the Gurdwara, to the men and women who do Guruji's work.

PAL: I've had a good few months haven't I Mum?

MAJOR: Oh yeah?

PAL: You see it pays to think strategically. Be open to new ideas.

LIZ: Reema's been doing the late shifts. She's been working really long hours haven't you Ree?

PAL: I've been training her.

REEMA: Training for what? I sit on the till, drink coca cola, moan about Wayne Rooney with the mentally ill goreh.

LIZ and COOKIE laugh.

PAL: Good honest work that is. Hard work.

REEMA: Teaching is far more challenging. Now that is hard work Birji.

LIZ: Bet you were a great teacher. Really caring.

REEMA: I was okay.

PAL: No money in teaching though is there?

Buoyant PAL hugs his mum.

PAL: Best start to the year we've ever had!

LIZ: Mum, you could at least say well done!

JEETO: *(Exasperated.)* Well done. Well done. Congratulations. You are the best. Okay. Happy now?

REEMA starts pouring out cups of tea onto trays. JEETO inspects the trays and addresses PAL and MAJOR.

JEETO: Offer the men first.

REEMA hands a tray to PAL, another to MAJOR. They exit. JEETO adjusts her chooni.

JEETO: I'll go and ask Gianiji if he needs anything more.

COOKIE: *(To REEMA.)* The last time she did that he went home with the microwave.

JEETO: Cookie, you come with me.

COOKIE: Why do I have to?

JEETO: To pay your respects.

COOKIE: Mum! He's…weird.

JEETO: Chull! *[get a move on!]*

COOKIE finds her chooni [scarf]. JEETO scans the kitchen area. Eyes LIZ.

JEETO: If I had left the sink like this, my mother-in-law would have cut my throat.

LIZ: I'm doing it!

JEETO and COOKIE exit. REEMA smiles at LIZ. As they talk, they clear up and put the furniture back into place.

REEMA: Have you spoken to Birji yet?

LIZ: Not yet. But he won't say no, not now he's in the money. I mean he can't, can he?

REEMA: Of course not.

LIZ stops, touches her tummy.

LIZ: Can you imagine feeling that little thing ticking inside you. You know I've already planned how I'll tell Pal, if…if it finally happens.

REEMA: You mean if you find out you're pregnant?

LIZ: I'll book a table for two at The Mandarin, and arrange it with the manager beforehand so when the waiter lifts the lid off the crispy duck, my pregnancy test will be sitting on top of the pancakes.

REEMA: But won't you have urinated on the test?

LIZ: Pal won't mind. He'll be over the moon when he sees them two lines.

REEMA: I see.

LIZ: Me and Pal, perfect in every way. Except…this one… The doctors call it unexplained. I reckon, this way…well, it might be the only way…

REEMA: You should talk to Pal Birji.

LIZ: Oh I will.

REEMA: Talk to him soon. You're a good person Liz. You shouldn't miss your moment.

LIZ: *(Pensive.)* No. *(A beat.)* Hey, you'll have to help me when it's born.

REEMA: Oh…I don't know anything about babies.

LIZ: I always wanted to be a young mum. And I'm not as young as I'd like but I'd hate to be one of them old ones. I see them every day picking the kids up from nursery. They're so worried about everything, tired and scared cos they know what life's really like. I don't wanna know about all that yet. D'you know what I mean?

REEMA: I don't want children.

LIZ: Course you do!

REEMA: I've never…I mean I don't feel…maternal…

LIZ: Only cos that Jiti put you off. Who'd wanna reproduce with him?

REEMA: He wasn't a bad man. But he was already married to the bottle.

LIZ: Like Daddy.

REEMA: Drink gave Jiti the freedom to dream. Always dreaming he was, anything to get away from the routine.

He hated all the chores Papaji made him do, hated the
farm…he just wanted something different…

LIZ: Right.

REEMA: I understand him better now I'm here.

LIZ: How's that?

REEMA: See the power you people have running your shop!

LIZ: Us lot?

REEMA: Sometimes…I wonder if I could do something else…
go to another place…

LIZ: Like where.

REEMA: America.

LIZ: You mean teach out there?

REEMA: I've had enough of working for others. One day…I'd
like to set up my own business. Possibly…a bookshop.

LIZ: Oh, I can see you doing that.

REEMA: Honestly?

LIZ: For sure. You're a big hit with Pal's customers and you've
always got your nose in a novel.

REEMA: But I would need more qualifications, capital. My
own money.

LIZ: Money isn't everything.

REEMA: You think?

LIZ: You can still be poor and happy.

REEMA: Then why don't you try it? Poor people are just the
rich people who never happened. The ones who didn't
take their chances. They end up passing time dreaming
dreams that never come true. Wasting days and weeks,
years.

LIZ: Are you serious about going?

REEMA: *(Nods.)* If I could get a job here first, I could pay for a
course.

LIZ: You're working in the shop.

REEMA: A proper job. With a salary. If I had my own money I could pay Thyji rent, contribute to the bills. Save up for my MBA.

LIZ: You should tell Mum. Her and Cookie have been looking on the internet at boys for you.

REEMA: *(Shocked.)* Boys?

LIZ: Men I should say. Most are divorced.

REEMA: So they won't mind second-hand goods.

LIZ: Haven't they mentioned it?

REEMA shakes her head. Landline rings. LIZ answers it.

LIZ: Hello… Oh Sat Siri Akal Chachaji. Yes it's Liz. Lij. Lij! Pal's wife. How are you?… Pal's wife!…Liz!…Hang on, I'll get her.

REEMA: Can I talk to him?

LIZ hands her the phone and calls out of the door.

LIZ: Mum, phone call from India!

REEMA: Sat siri akal Papaji… Hahji… I miss you. Hah…yes, I am happy…but it's different… Hahji, how are you…

She continues talking quietly in Punjabi. JEETO enters followed by PAL who carries a stack of thalis.

LIZ: Chacha.

JEETO takes the phone from REEMA.

JEETO: *(To LIZ.)* Bathroom needs cleaning.

LIZ: What?

PAL: Binder's been sick.

LIZ: *(Heading out.)* Can't leave the work surfaces like that Reema, Mum'll start to self-harm.

LIZ exits. PAL hands REEMA the thalis. He tidies away as she washes up.

JEETO: *(Shouts into phone.)* Hahnji. Sat siri akal... Hah...
Everybody came...

PAL: Will you stop shouting?

JEETO: *(To PAL.)* He is in India stupid! *(Into phone.)* Hahji... Oh
Reema is fine. Working hard for the family... Very good
girl... No, you cannot have her back... Acha... Acha... I
see... Okay... I understand... Don't worry... I will talk to
him... we will send you by the end of next week... Don't
worry. Hahji... Hah... Everybody came... Hah... Sat siri
Akal...

She replaces the phone.

PAL: Send what by the end of next week?

JEETO ignores him, busies herself tidying up.

PAL: Send what?

JEETO: The kauthee *[house]* needs rewiring.

PAL: The whole house?

JEETO: Yes.

PAL: But that's gonna cost a fortune!

JEETO: You've just been telling the whole world how much
money you're making.

PAL: I'm not working day and night to chuck my profits down
the black hole Chacha's digging for himself.

JEETO: Your Chacha needs our help.

PAL: He must be earning something from the land.

JEETO: Whatever he earns goes to pay his debts.

PAL: Why is he holding on to the land then?

REEMA: Because it's all he has left. You don't know what it's
like over there.

PAL: Who's asking you?

REEMA: I'm just saying you don't know.

PAL: I know I'm maintaining a house I'm never gonna live in.

JEETO: I'm going to live there. One day.

PAL: What for?

JEETO: To be close to my relatives.

PAL: Come on Mum, they're all dead. Or living in Mississauga. *(A beat.)* Now Chacha's on his own, he can't cope. That house and that land's draining away everything we've got.

JEETO: You think when you fall on hard times, you give up? When Daddy died and you took over the shop and lost us money did I give up on you? No you stupid bloody bastard, I saved you! That land, that jameen, is Daddy's blood. Your blood. It's all that matters. And you fight to save what matters.

PAL: Thing is I turned it around Mum, I'm making more money than Daddy ever was. Maybe you just don't know when to stop fighting.

Silence. JEETO starts making more tea.

PAL: Uncle Hothi was saying a lot of people round here are selling their shares of land back home.

JEETO: Your blood has farmed that land for centuries. Now you want to hand it over to some stranger.

PAL: Who said anything about handing it over? And it doesn't have to be to a stranger. Bet there's someone in the village who could use it. Someone who's gonna be there and help Chacha. Think about it, if you sell your share…

JEETO: Sell my hissa?

PAL: Do something more interesting with the money. You're a sleeping partner Mum, you're no use to Chacha.

JEETO: Did I teach my son to talk like this?

PAL: It'll still be our jameen *[land]*. Chacha's not going anywhere is he?

REEMA: If you sell, the money lenders will get their claws into Papaji's land, bleed him for every rupee.

PAL: You don't know that! Mum, you could still go and visit, stay for as long as you like.

JEETO: Your daddy always said we would go back home, me and him. We'd visit all the Gurdwaras in the Punjab. Make our lives in that house.

PAL: He never went back Mum. Not once!

JEETO: That jameen, that house, is the memory of the future I should have had with your daddy. It's all I have left of him.

PAL: Then do what you want. Land's in your name. You do what you want with it.

JEETO: How did you learn to think like this?

PAL: What do you mean?

JEETO: Like a gorah. Talking like your chacha and your daddy mean nothing.

PAL: I'm not.

The fury rises within JEETO.

JEETO: You want to sell your daddy's land? Sell my land? To some haramzada nobody? Who do you think you are talking to? The next thing you'll say is you want to sell the shop.

PAL turns to face her.

PAL: I've sold it.

JEETO freezes. REEMA stares at PAL. Silence.

PAL: Haven't exchanged contracts yet but that's a formality.

JEETO: You...sold the shop?

PAL: My shop Mum. It's my business. Daddy put it in my name, remember?

Shocked JEETO sits down. She blankly turns to REEMA.

JEETO: Go and see if our guests need anything more.

REEMA exits. Silence. JEETO composes herself.

JEETO: Does Cookie know?

PAL: Nothing to do with Cookie.

JEETO: Do you know what it took for your daddy to own that shop?

PAL: Yeah.

JEETO: Why?

PAL: Cos I hate it. I've always hated it. Wandering round that Cash and Carry makes me want to kill myself! Checking and filling that stinking stock room… And waiting at that till like somebody's servant, having to be grateful that they're spending a couple of quid…people looking at me, talking to me like I'm a moron, some pindoo *[villager]* without a brain cell.

JEETO: Is that what you think of us?

PAL: It's what they think of us.

JEETO: Me and Daddy used to work 80 hours a week. Every morning getting goreh newspapers ready. Every night being breathed on by drunks. In the end he was so stressed…and tired… And you show no thanks. That man gave his life for you.

PAL: For me?

JEETO: Hah *[yes]*.

PAL: Daddy died because he drank too much.

JEETO: When a man works that hard he needs something to ease his mind.

PAL: Every night he'd sip his Bacardi bottle till the room started to spin. Then he'd start crying and want a hug and start singing *(Sings.)* 'Peenee peenee peenee peenee eh sharab.' *['Drink, drink, drink booze.']* An hour later you'd be walking around with a bucket of Dettol, mopping up his sick and piss.

JEETO: We made sacrifices so that you could have your life.

PAL: I'd come home from school with a love bite or homework or bruises on my face and you'd be stuck in that stock room counting tins of beans. You never bothered to talk to me or Cookie.

JEETO: So you are selling the shop because nobody talked to you? Are you a man or a little girl?

PAL: I didn't ask for any of it Mum. You just thought I wanted what you wanted. But you never asked me. I could have taken exams, gone to college even…

JEETO: Oh yes, because your grades were so good!

PAL: If I hadn't spent every school night behind that till they might have been better. You never paid any attention to what I was capable of. I could be working in the City now. Making a fortune…

JEETO: So we didn't make enough money for you? You had – DVD players, computers, games…anything you asked for. We let you marry your goree.

PAL: Is that what you think of her?

JEETO: No, it's what I think of you!

PAL sits down, tired of the argument.

JEETO: He put the shop in your name because he trusted you. He gave you the power…

PAL: Daddy never gave me no power. I took it. He would have done the same.

JEETO: *(A beat.)* Pal. *(A beat.)* Don't sell his shop. Please.

LIZ enters cautiously. She's carrying trays.

PAL: I'm building a nursing home. With Harj. We've been talking about it for months. Been to the bank with the business plan and they've said yes. We're gonna renovate a pub. The King George. Daddy used to go there on a Friday night when we were kids. Remember? It's like a cemetery now. We're starting small but we know what we want. There's a load of money in care homes Mum. I can do this. I want to show you…

JEETO gets up. LIZ starts clearing the trays. JEETO walks out. PAL composes a text on his phone.

LIZ: Do you think she's alright?

PAL: She'll get used to it.

LIZ: At least she's still got us lot.

PAL: Yeah.

> *PAL is checking his phone. He gets a text.*

LIZ: Pal…

PAL: I'll see you later.

LIZ: Hang on…

PAL: *(Heading out.)* I'm meeting Harj.

LIZ: Wait…

PAL: He's got an uncle in India who might want to invest.

LIZ: Please! There's no time to talk to you any more.

> *He stops.*

LIZ: It's just…now you're doing so well, I thought…

PAL: What?

LIZ: I thought…maybe…we could have a think, about that IVF. I got some leaflets and…

PAL: *(Interrupts.)* You're not still on about that are you?

LIZ: We didn't have the money before.

PAL: I need every penny for the business, you know I do.

LIZ: But it's what I want. And now you've sold the shop, Mum's gonna need something, she deserves something…

PAL: What the hell's it got to do with Mum?

LIZ: It's everything to do with her!

PAL: She's putting ideas into your head!

LIZ: Mum wants us to be happy.

PAL: We are fucking happy! *(A beat.)* Let's see where we are after the home's up and running. Yeah?

> *No response.*

PAL: You're stressing yourself out Liz.

LIZ: It's not about the money is it?

PAL: I told you it is.

LIZ: Liar.

PAL: I've never lied to you. Never once in my life.

LIZ: You don't want a baby.

PAL: *(Exasperated.)* Fucking hell.

LIZ: Not like I do. What's the point of us?

PAL: Eh?

LIZ: What's the point of me being here? If you don't want the thing I can't live without. *(A beat.)* All I ever wanted was to get married and have kids.

PAL: I've gotta go.

He exits. LIZ watches him leave.

SCENE FOUR (JUNE)

JEETO sits on the armchair with her feet in the basin. She is half listening to the radio. She takes out the photo of her husband, beholds it lovingly.

The song 'Main Shayar To Nahin' from the film Bobby *comes on.*

Suddenly JEETO begins doing part of the notorious dance performed by Helen in the film. She does the moves perfectly and performs the love song to the photo of her husband. The song ends.

She turns off the radio and sits back down, dries her feet. COOKIE enters, talking on the phone, she's dressed in designer jeans, immaculately made up and carries a large tote. As she's talking, she takes out a laptop and sets it up on the table.

COOKIE: She's twelve, so it's got to be the shape of a twelve...I dunno do I? Whatever shape a twelve is!... Pink... Yeah... All the shades of pink you've got... Happy Birthday Princess Simmy... Not Simply!... Simmy!... All capitals...and tasteful yeah, none of that spidery lettering... S.I.M.M.Y... Y not I. Y... Alright...yeah...next week. Bye.

JEETO: Simmy must be excited about her party.

COOKIE: She's not bothered. Dunno why I'm bothering. We made do with a Victoria Sandwich from the stock room. Remember?

JEETO: Chah bunah *[make the tea]*.

COOKIE goes to put the tea on.

COOKIE: If you scroll down there's a cardiac surgeon and a couple of accountants. They're not catwalk material but then she's hardly Miss India.

JEETO: *(On laptop.)* The surgeon is aged seventy-five.

COOKIE: Well Reema's no spring chicken.

JEETO: And this accountant lives in Bangladesh. He is a mussulman *[muslim]* you stupid!

COOKIE: Major said he'd come back with Pal. What time is he normally home?

JEETO: Who knows? He lives on that building site.

COOKIE: Well he wants to make a success of it. And he's helping us out. I mean this contract for the bathrooms has given Major's business a proper boost.

JEETO: He never needed help before.

COOKIE: It's hard for builders these days. You don't know what these Polish cowboys are like. Major can't compete with their prices. *(A beat.)* Any word from Liz?

JEETO: She is still at her parents.

COOKIE: But she is coming back?

JEETO: Ask your brother.

COOKIE: You look tired Mum.

JEETO: My daughter-in-law should be here.

COOKIE: Isn't that Reema supposed to be keeping you company?

JEETO: She is helping Pal build his bloody home.

COOKIE: You can't blame him for wanting to do his own thing.

JEETO: *(On laptop.)* Funeral Director. Divorced. Bald. Good teeth.

COOKIE: She'll say no to bald.

JEETO: That girl is too fussy.

COOKIE: That's what I should have been.

COOKIE brings over tea and biscuits.

COOKIE: Has he shown you the pictures of the nursing home?

JEETO: On his bloody iPad.

COOKIE: Hasn't skimped on the decor has he? Always thought I was the one with the taste. But cream and mauve do work. Rooms look so fresh…

JEETO: Once the old people come the place will start to smell.

COOKIE: You're so bloody ungrateful, he's doing all this for you!

JEETO: I don't want to live in his smelly rooms. He can keep his gorah business! Old people should be looked after at home by their children.

COOKIE: He's gonna make more money than Daddy ever dreamed of.

JEETO: How much money do we need?

COOKIE: I dunno, more than we've got.

JEETO: I won't be here to spend it. You can't build a house with broken bricks. And if you do, the cracks will show.

COOKIE: You wanna stop watching that Star TV.

JEETO: I've told Chacha, and I have booked my ticket for December. One way. After I leave you will never see me again.

COOKIE: *(Sighs.)* I doubt that.

JEETO: What am I staying here for?

REEMA enters. Puts her bag down.

JEETO: Daddy put the business in Pal's name. I put this house in Pal's name. And I still have no grandson to look after.

COOKIE: You've got two granddaughters.

JEETO: I'm going back to my land, to rest my eyes on green fields.

REEMA: There are green fields here.

JEETO: People here don't love the land like they do back home.

REEMA: Love sometimes turns to hate.

JEETO: *(Indicates the laptop.)* Funeral director. Good teeth.

REEMA: *(Glances at the screen.)* Acha *[I see].*

JEETO: Time is running out Kurreeh.

REEMA: Time?

JEETO: You need to choose somebody. Soon.

COOKIE: *(To REEMA.)* Have you finished that course?

REEMA: I passed the NVQ Level One.

COOKIE: Get you, brainbox! I failed all my GCSEs. Is he gonna make you clean the toilets?

REEMA: No, the cleaner will do that.

JEETO: Indian girls have changed. They used to be glad to just be doing something. Did you know I cleaned toilets when I first came to this country?

COOKIE: Oh, where the hell is Major?

JEETO gets up, observes her hands.

JEETO: These hands won't clean toilets again. No sir! *(Gets up.)* Pushaab ondhe *[my wee is coming].* Reema, roti bunah *[make the roti].*

She exits. REEMA takes out an iPad Mini, opens it and starts typing.

COOKIE: Where did you get that?

REEMA: Birji asked me to check his accounts.

COOKIE: Why?

REEMA: Probably because I am good at mathematics and he doesn't have to pay me.

COOKIE: Right little mover and shaker aren't you?

REEMA goes to the kitchen, starts making roti.

COOKIE: Here's the invite to Simmy's do. *(Shows her.)* I've got caterers so us lot can relax and enjoy ourselves.

REEMA: Thought it was a children's party.

COOKIE: Yeah, but I've still booked a DJ and there'll be cava.

REEMA: I wasn't planning to come.

COOKIE: What do you mean?

REEMA: Why give them more to gossip about. Anyway won't be much fun without Liz.

COOKIE: Can't have everyone thinking we lock you up in the kitchen. And wear something decent. Buy a new suit.

REEMA: I don't have any money.

COOKIE reaches for the biscuit jar.

COOKIE: Daddy always made sure Mum had her emergency fund. *(Rummages.)* Is a hundred enough?

REEMA nods. COOKIE passes her the notes.

COOKIE: If it's not, tell me and I'll sort you out.

REEMA holds the money. She stares at it.

REEMA: I want…my own money…

COOKIE: You have been staying here for free.

REEMA: Free?

An angry REEMA shows COOKIE her floured hands.

REEMA: Since Liz went, who irons the clothes, washes the floor, cooks each meal? Who boils the water for your constant, endless bloody chah…you people have more chah running through your veins than blood!

COOKIE: Mum's trying to help you move on. Why do you think she's on Shaadi dot com every night? Least you get to choose. I never.

REEMA: You have a nice family. Big house, expensive car. Good business. In India, a girl might kill for your life.

COOKIE: Mum was always gonna find you a husband. She's giving you a leg-up back into the community. If that wasn't what you wanted, you shouldn't have come…

REEMA: This is the UK, I thought you understood about freedom.

COOKIE: Freedom? You have to make do. Get on with it, like everyone else.

REEMA: You can turn all your dreams into reality. Anything you want you get because you can pay for it!

COOKIE: You think I'm that shallow?

COOKIE takes over, starts making roti.

REEMA: What could there be Bhanji, that you don't have?

COOKIE: You said it love, I'm the chick who's got it all.

REEMA: Some people become accustomed to dissatisfaction.

COOKIE: Like I said, best to get on with it.

REEMA: What I don't understand is, why they don't change the circumstance of such dissatisfaction?

COOKIE: *(Stops.)* Expect it's like planting a bomb. On your life.

REEMA: I wish there were bombs being planted all over the world!

COOKIE takes vegetables out. Begins chopping. REEMA watches her.

REEMA: I'd like my own place.

COOKIE: Good luck. Go if you want.

REEMA: With two pounds in my pocket?

COOKIE: You're here for Mum until she finds you the right man. That's what Chacha thinks.

REEMA: What's this got to do with Chacha?

COOKIE: You're still his daughter-in-law. You leave this house and that's his izzat gone. His honour's all he's got left.

REEMA: I know about his honour.

COOKIE: Suppose you're not likely to see him again, so it doesn't matter.

REEMA: Chacha matters.

COOKIE: You're not even properly related, not by blood.

REEMA: Chacha is my family. *(Fierce.)* But you know, I have a right to be paid and to choose my future. *(A beat.)* Bhanji, you could ask Pal Birji for me.

COOKIE: Me?

REEMA: Stop one more woman from entering a circumstance she hates.

COOKIE: Nobody hands you life on a plate love. Ask him yourself.

REEMA: What would you do?

COOKIE: My time's gone…

REEMA: If you had your chance again…

COOKIE: *(A beat.)* I'd fucking grab it.

MAJOR and PAL enter.

MAJOR: Gonna be too cramped.

PAL: Shut up willya. Oy Reema, stick the chah on…

REEMA goes to make more tea. MAJOR's holding architect's plans.

MAJOR: Let me speak to the architect, if you add an extra 240mill…

PAL: They don't need a wash every day.

MAJOR: Who?

PAL: Old people.

COOKIE: Why not?

PAL: Tires them out.

MAJOR unfolds the plans, shows PAL.

MAJOR: There'll be a carer in there as well, I'm telling you, the extra 240'll make all the difference.

PAL: It's not the Ritz. Me and Harj looked round loads of care homes, the bathrooms are designed like that.

MAJOR: I've seen bigger kennels.

PAL: Regulation spec, the architect said.

MAJOR: There should be a certain amount of space between the toilet and the sink…

PAL: *(Interrupts.)* We need to get six residents on both floors.

MAJOR: What you charging per week?

PAL: Depends on their individual needs.

REEMA: Starts at seven hundred.

MAJOR: Seven hundred pounds?

PAL: Specialised care for Asians isn't it? All the carers speak the languages. Food's Gujarati or Punjabi. I'll even set a few fireworks off at Diwali. Reckon we can charge up to twelve fifty.

MAJOR: You're looking at more than ten grand a week.

REEMA: Income not profit. There are overheads, staff and associated costs.

MAJOR: Right.

COOKIE: She's got an iPad.

PAL: *(To COOKIE.)* Will you tell him?

COOKIE: *(To MAJOR.)* Just do what he says.

MAJOR: What do you know about fitting bathrooms? These plans aren't right.

PAL: If you don't want the job there's plenty who do.

COOKIE: Course he wants the job.

REEMA serves the tea.

PAL: They'll have enough space to soak their dentures. Come on Major, I want them to be happy, why do you think I'm doing this? *(Drinks tea.)* You'll make a packet.

MAJOR: Okay…okay.

Resigned MAJOR puts the plans down.

COOKIE: Who's doing your website?

PAL: Harj has sorted it. Reema'll show you.

REEMA shows them on the iPad. COOKIE and MAJOR are impressed.

COOKIE: Told you he knew what he was doing.

PAL: We've already had enquiries.

MAJOR: My bank manager said they weren't lending.

PAL: Business plan was spot on wasn't it Reema? And I had the capital from the shop.

MAJOR: This is a different league to the shop.

COOKIE: What did Harj put in?

PAL: His house.

MAJOR: His house?

PAL: As security.

COOKIE: Harj's house and the shop aren't enough to finance this business.

PAL: The bank gave us the mortgage to buy the pub. And we got an additional investor to fund the refurb.

COOKIE: Who?

PAL: Harj's Uncle Manjit. From India.

MAJOR: He's got this kind of money?

PAL: Uncle Manjit's Mr Big in telecoms in Amritsar. He reckons the future's in nursing homes. He likes us and the idea, wants to stay in the background while we do the leg work. Says we'll all make a fortune. And we will.

COOKIE: *(Impressed.)* You've worked out all your costings haven't you.

PAL: Course. Bank wouldn't have agreed to lend us otherwise.

REEMA indicates a page on the iPad.

REEMA: Staff/resident ratios, figures for the food and the domestics.

PAL: Show them the rota of nurses, there's a medical professional on duty twenty-four seven.

COOKIE: That's good innit Major…

REEMA: It's the law.

COOKIE: Sad though, packing all these budeh *[old people]* away like Christmas presents no one wants. I mean if you stuck Mum in there, she'd start a fire.

PAL: Not all Asian elders have kids to look after them. Even if they do, everyone's working nowadays. We can look after them properly, stop them getting lonely.

MAJOR: Haven't seen much of Liz lately.

PAL: Yeah, well…her mum's got…blood pressure.

MAJOR's phone rings. He answers it, goes off to the side.

PAL: *(To COOKIE.)* Hey, you'll have to organise a big do for the opening.

COOKIE: Leave it to me.

PAL: I know what people are saying. They're all watching to see what I do after the shop, waiting for me to trip up. They'll be waiting a long time. *(Finds papers.)* I wanna show Mum the letterhead. *(Shows cookies.)* See, they put my name on it and everything. *(Heads out.)* Bring some more chah up Reema.

He exits. REEMA gets a tea tray ready. MAJOR comes off the phone. COOKIE observes her husband.

COOKIE: Who was that?

MAJOR: Simmy, she's nervous about the party. Too much pressure…

REEMA exits.

COOKIE: I'm the one doing everything.

MAJOR: She needed to talk.

COOKIE: She never talks to me.

MAJOR: You're busy.

COOKIE: If you do a good job on these bathrooms you might get another contract. I could get a manager in the salon. Full-time. Then I can be at home more.

MAJOR: You hate being at home.

COOKIE's phone rings, it's on the table near MAJOR, he picks it up.

COOKIE: Wait, I'll answer it!

He answers it.

MAJOR: Hello…hello…

The other person rings off. MAJOR looks down at the phone. REEMA comes back in.

MAJOR: Your mate Tracey… Funny how she never wants to speak to me.

They stare at each other. He chucks the phone to her.

MAJOR: I'll meet you in the car.

He exits. COOKIE and REEMA exchange a look. REEMA clears up the tea tray.

COOKIE: Think you're noble do you? Sacrificing your life for Chacha.

REEMA: You know all about sacrifice Bhanji.

COOKIE: I never sacrificed anything love. I just didn't have the bottle to do what I wanted. I've turned an old barber's into the tackiest beauty salon in town. I've fed and clothed two kids who hate my guts. And I'm walking around on the arm of a man who I've never loved. That's my lot. Thing is I've got too much personality to feel sorry for myself.

COOKIE gets her bag.

COOKIE: I say, if your life's over why not kill yourself?

PAL comes back in.

PAL: Any more chah going?

REEMA goes to get him more tea. He composes a text. COOKIE eyes REEMA.

COOKIE: There's always a chink of light. If there wasn't, you wouldn't be breathing in and out.

COOKIE exits. REEMA watches her go. PAL reads through papers. REEMA slowly makes PAL's tea, takes it to him. Suddenly the cup falls from her hands to the floor.

PAL: What's wrong with you?

He clears it up.

REEMA: I'm sorry.

PAL: Uncle Manjit wants to see the copy for the brochure. We need to flag up the prayer room, outline dementia provision, mention the activities coordinator, that sort of thing.

He indicates the papers. REEMA stares at him.

REEMA: What do you think will happen to me, when you make a success of the home?

PAL: Dunno.

REEMA: I'm helping you for nothing.

PAL: You're living here for nothing.

REEMA: I deserve something. I must do.

PAL: Like what?

REEMA: When the home opens and the money comes, I want you to give me a loan for my MBA.

PAL: You that desperate for letters after your name?

REEMA: I'll pay you back. I swear. But I need to know.

PAL: *(A beat.)* Reckon you've earned it.

REEMA: You promise?

PAL: I'm not bothered what you do, as long as you pay me back.

REEMA: Thank you Birji...thank you... Knowing there's something to aim for makes a difference. *(Takes the papers.)*

PAL: Right.

REEMA: And doing a course like that, will give me chance. Being my own boss, it's what I've always wanted.

PAL: Lucky you.

REEMA: *(Flicks through papers.)* Your name on the letterhead, isn't that what you always wanted?

PAL: Yeah.

REEMA goes to make more tea.

REEMA: There's no sugar left.

PAL: Eh?

REEMA: Liz usually does the shopping.

PAL: Forget it.

He goes to the kitchen, finds a bottle of whisky.

REEMA: You must miss her. We all do.

He pours a glass, downs it.

PAL: Liz isn't interested in the business.

REEMA: Of course she is. You strike gold with the nursing home and she'll be here again, where she belongs.

He pours himself another glass.

REEMA: Are you listening? This house is Liz's house. You must find a way to get her. What about Simmy's party? Yes, that's it. You call her and tell her and she'll come. She'll come for Simmy.

PAL: I dunno.

REEMA: What do you mean you don't know?

PAL downs his drink.

REEMA: You've got to fight!

PAL: Maybe…maybe I can't have both. I mean Liz and the business…

REEMA: *(Interrupts.)* Harj's uncle is a multi-millionaire, and he believes in you. In this concept. He's chosen to invest in you and Harj. If it's not you, it'll be someone else. Could you bear that? *(A beat.)* You'll make more money in two years than your father made in his lifetime.

She and PAL stare at each other.

REEMA: Call her now. Invite her to Simmy's party.

She finds his phone, thrusts it into his hand.

REEMA: This is your chance. Take it!

PAL contemplates the phone. Lights down.

INTERVAL

ACT TWO

SCENE ONE (JUNE)

SIMMY's party. Bhangra music plays. Flashing lights. All the characters are dressed up to the nines and they dance enthusiastically. Music fades and they form a huddle around a huge cake. They all start singing Happy Birthday to SIMMY. The party goes on. To fade. Lights go down...

SCENE TWO

Later the same night, PAL and LIZ enter the Gill living room. He's wearing his suit from the party. LIZ is wearing a glam shalwar kameez also from the party. They are a bit tentative with each other, almost as if it's a first date.

PAL: Do you want a drink?

LIZ: Water please.

He pours her a glass of water, makes himself a large whisky.

LIZ: D'you think Simmy enjoyed herself?

PAL: Yeah, why not?

LIZ: She was sick in the toilets.

PAL: So was I.

Gives her the drink.

PAL: Thanks for coming. Meant a lot to Mum and Cookie.

LIZ: What about you?

PAL: Course me. *(Beholds her.)* You're beautiful you know that?

LIZ: *(Indicates her Kameez.)* Oh, I love this suit. Daddy bought it from Southall for me, after we got engaged. Remember?

PAL: I'm not talking about the suit.

LIZ moves away shyly.

LIZ: Reema said you're working together.

PAL: She's helping me out, with the home, you know.

LIZ: Makes sense. Reema's bright as a button.

PAL: She's hoping you'll be here in the morning. We all are.

Coy LIZ looks around the room.

LIZ: Feels strange being back.

PAL: Feels right to me. Been like me arm's missing.

LIZ: Stupid.

PAL: Nothing works without you. Never has. Since that first time I asked you to dance. Still can't believe you said yes.

LIZ: They were playing all them old tunes.

PAL: Teacher's favourites. So what if I asked you again now?

LIZ: Depends on the song.

PAL: Same one as back then. Just like I'm the same.

LIZ: You sure about that?

PAL: You know I am.

LIZ: What you waiting for?

PAL: Elizabeth Bradley, I've watched you singing in assembly, writing in history and titrating in chemistry. I know I'm a bit pissed but will you give me a dance? Please beautiful, perfect Elizabeth Bradley, one dance and I'll never bother you again.

He holds out his hand, she takes it.

LIZ: So you really want me to stay?

PAL: Never wanted you to go. *(Holds her close/Kisses her.)*

He turns the iPad on. 'True' by Spandau Ballet starts to play. They dance, it's as if they're back at the school disco where they first danced. They dance and kiss, dance and kiss. His phone rings. He turns it off, chucks it on a table. They carry on dancing. Suddenly the music is interrupted by a ping on the iPad which indicates receipt of an email. PAL stops when he hears the sound, but the music resumes and he goes back to dancing. They dance. Suddenly PAL breaks away from LIZ. He picks up the iPad, music stops, he checks his email.

LIZ: Pal!

PAL: Sorry, I just need to check something.

LIZ: I don't believe this!

PAL: I'll only be a minute.

LIZ: Can't you ever put that thing down!

PAL: I will, hold on…

LIZ: I wanna go to bed.

PAL: So do I.

LIZ: Come on then!

PAL: *(Reading.)* Harj needs some figures for tomorrow.

LIZ: *(Pointing at iPad.)* That thing, your bloody nursing home, won't make you happy.

PAL: After it's set up, we can afford to do anything, go anywhere. To the Maldives, I'll buy you a Maserati, you'll never have to lift a finger as long as you live.

LIZ: I'm ovulating!

PAL: We'll do it in the morning.

LIZ: I have to be at work at eight.

PAL: Won't take long.

LIZ: I need to lie still afterwards for at least half an hour.

PAL: Half an hour?

LIZ: So there's a chance of fertilisation.

PAL: *(Stops.)* Is that what you came back for?

No response.

PAL: *(Fierce.)* I asked you a question!

LIZ: Everywhere I go, I see mums pushing buggies, handing snacks to toddlers on them scooters. And on the news, they go on about how much ribena they can have and how you should read them fairy tales after bathtime. I could do that. I know about all that. I just need a chance.

PAL goes to the kitchen, finds a bottle of whisky, pours himself a glass.

PAL: So…that's the only thing you want from me?

LIZ: *(Upset.)* It's all I can think about. Wish it wasn't. But it is.

PAL: Do you love me?

LIZ: Yes.

PAL: I mean like you used to?

LIZ: Course I do.

PAL: You're enough Liz, you always have been.

LIZ: *(A beat.)* I need more.

PAL: Than what?

Silence.

PAL: Go on, say it.

He approaches her.

PAL: I'm sorry. Let's go to bed.

LIZ: I should never have come back.

PAL: I love you. I've loved you from that first moment.

LIZ: *(A beat.)* This…this is rubbish, it's rubbish…I'd better go.

She exits.

PAL: Liz! *(Shouts.)* Liz!

PAL fights back tears, composes himself. Dressing-gown clad REEMA enters.

PAL: We were talking and then…she went.

PAL swigs from the bottle of whisky.

PAL: Can't she see the bags under my eyes? I mean I'm trying so fucking hard to make this work.

PAL finds another bottle of whisky, goes to leave.

REEMA: Birji…

PAL: What?

REEMA: That bottle won't change anything.

PAL: Thing is, it does. For a bit. *(A beat.)* Thanks.

He exits.

SCENE THREE (JULY)

Weeks later. Late evening. REEMA is on the iPad. JEETO is in the kitchen area. JEETO is serving up PAL's dinner. The atmosphere between the two women is heavy, tense. JEETO puts PAL's food on the table.

REEMA: Birji is late.

JEETO: What is there to come home for?

REEMA: Roti.

JEETO: Here is not like back home, men don't finish work when the sun sets. He has paperwork to do, internet, emails, Facebook, Google…

REEMA: Thyji, I told you we have computers in India.

JEETO: Hah, hah, hah *[yes, yes, yes]*, you know everything.

REEMA: And plenty of sharab in every pind. We don't need pubs for our men to be lost.

JEETO: You have been here long enough Kurreeh. Time you were married.

REEMA: I have work to do.

JEETO: Oh yes, no man is good enough for Reema! Is this how you were with Jiti? Moaning, groaning? It's up to a woman to keep hold of her man.

REEMA: That's not easy. You and me, we know.

JEETO: Kee?

REEMA: Both our husbands were drunks.

Suddenly JEETO stops dishing up.

JEETO: You're learning bad habits Kurreeh. Back home if a kurreeh like you talked this way to a budeeh *[old woman]* like me, that budeeh might kill her. Not with a knife or a pistol, but with one look from her eyes.

REEMA: Where is this back home you talk about? This place with green fields and the Pappar man and Gurdas Maan on the radio, where every day there is a wedding and ladies doing Gidha. In my Punjab, the men are running away from their birthrights, abandoning their women, drinking sharab *[alcohol]* all day and taking nusheh *[drugs]*, hanging themselves with their pugs *[turbans]*, because there's nothing. Nothing!

JEETO: When your heart is dark, all you see is darkness.

REEMA: And where is your light Thyji? Where is the light in this house?

JEETO: My daughter-in-law took it with her, the day she left.

PAL enters, he's on the phone.

PAL: Just tell him Harj… We can't have known, the survey said the electrics looked alright… Tell Uncle Manjit the subcontractor assured me it's gonna be fine, just might delay the alarm system by a few weeks… He's sent the first instalment hasn't he?… Gonna cost an extra few thousand that's all… Ok, yeah…you Skype him…tell him…tell him it's getting sorted.

He ends the call, opens his iPad, sets it up on the counter, starts typing.

JEETO: Roti?

PAL: Me and Harj had chips.

JEETO: Chips is not food.

PAL: Willya stop going on?

JEETO: You need to bring your wife home.

JEETO slowly gathers her bag and stuff together.

JEETO: Kurreeh, don't wake me in the morning.

She wearily heads to the door and goes upstairs. REEMA continues to clear the kitchen.

PAL: Dunno why the Indian's getting his Kachee in a twist.

REEMA: This is how it is. He wants to be kept informed.

PAL: He should trust us.

REEMA: Trust doesn't count in India, people believe in hard cash.

PAL: He's gonna get plenty of that.

REEMA: Harj's uncle knows. He's just making you sweat.

PAL: Yeah.

REEMA: Do you want to eat?

PAL: Later.

He gets up and goes to pour a drink from a bottle of Johnnie Walker Black Label. REEMA watches him.

REEMA: Can I have some?

PAL: What?

REEMA: Can I have a drink? Whisky.

PAL: Help yourself.

REEMA finds a glass, pours herself a drink. She downs it. PAL sits, continues to work on the iPad. REEMA fills her glass with more whisky.

PAL: Didn't realise you drank.

REEMA: My husband taught me. Do you remember him?

PAL: A bit.

REEMA: Jiti used to talk about you all the time. He looked up to you, like an older brother.

PAL: Me?

REEMA: He told me about the fun you had when he visited you all. Bowling, cinema, you watched *Matrix* didn't you?

PAL: Right, yeah.

REEMA: There is a photo of you and him together on Chacha's mantelpiece. From your day trip to London.

PAL: Oh yeah, we went to Buckingham Palace.

REEMA: No, it was the Tower of London. Don't you remember?

PAL: Was ages ago.

REEMA: Jiti said you used to have long talks.

PAL: Dunno.

REEMA: When he and Chacha argued, he would always say nobody understands me, except Pal Birji.

PAL: Did he?

REEMA: Chacha also thinks a lot of you. And your mum. He said you would look after me. Have you heard from Liz?

PAL stops for a second, then carries on typing.

REEMA: When they go, it's like they take your future with them.

REEMA pours more drinks.

REEMA: You know when Jiti left, I could have gone back to my own village, to my parents.

PAL: Why didn't you?

REEMA: Chacha.

PAL: He could have got a servant to clean the house and make roti.

REEMA: My parents were never interested in me. My sister was more beautiful and my brother was...the son made of gold. But after I was married Chacha treated me like I was his blood. He was the father I should have had.

PAL: *(Amused.)* What are you on about?

REEMA: After the home opens, I'd like to move out. I'll still work for you, hopefully...I'll be starting my course. But... you see, I'm worried about Chacha.

PAL: Once Mum's out there, she'll be making his roti, and I'll send her a few quid every month, whatever she needs, so Chacha's gonna be fine.

REEMA: It's not that.

PAL: What then?

REEMA: *(A beat.)* Can I tell you something?... Something I haven't told anyone.

PAL nods. REEMA watches PAL uneasily, walks round the room with her drink. Stops.

REEMA: Once, before Jiti left, he had been playing cards with some men from the village. He lost the game and owed them money.

Late one night I was sleeping and these men came to the kauthee *[house]*. They wanted their money but Jiti had gone out drinking, he was taking nushih *[drugs]* by then. I heard Chacha's voice and shouting on the verandah. I got out of bed and went outside. The men were drunk and one of them grabbed me, the others laughed and this man started pulling at my clothes, Chacha shouted at them to stop but they wouldn't.

I was screaming. Chacha went inside. They carried on laughing and…my hair came loose. The next thing I knew, there was a noise like a bomb and the man, the one who was holding me, fell back. I looked up and there was Chacha with his rifle. He shouted at them to go, to stay away from his land. The others took the dead one and went. They never came back. Chacha started crying and cursing Jiti. He said, you are my daughter now kureeh *[girl]*. You are my izzat and I am yours. We will protect each other's honour.

PAL: Chacha killed a man?

REEMA: He did the right thing. And I swore I would do the right thing by him. But now…if I leave here, his izzat will be destroyed. *(A beat.)* He is owed better than that. *(Drinks.)* I don't know what to do.

PAL: I'm sorry.

REEMA: Why should you know? All you consider is your self-advancement.

REEMA pours more drinks. They are both getting steadily drunker.

PAL: Is that what you think of me? I bathed my dad the last year of his life. Carried him to the toilet and dressed him every day so he could die at home. Even passed him a Johnnie Walker miniature so he had a smile on his deathbed. He told me to take care of the shop. To look after Mum and Liz. *(Drinks.)* My Dad and Chacha and all that lot, they have these expectations, you have to leave them behind.

REEMA: How do you learn to bear their disappointment?

69

PAL: Just…get used to it.

REEMA: It's different for you. Because you are a male. *(Takes his hand.)* We are both flesh and blood, see. We should be the same.

PAL: We are.

REEMA: Both drunk.

They laugh.

REEMA: Worth the same I mean. I want to be worth the same, as you.

PAL: You can decide what you're worth.

REEMA: Can I?

PAL: It's not a decision you should let other people make.

REEMA: *(Drinks.)* Didn't you ever want something different?

PAL: Had everything I wanted here. Thought I did.

REEMA: And you never want to escape?

PAL: Yeah. Yeah sometimes I do now.

REEMA: I don't think there's anything wrong with wanting more.

PAL: More?

REEMA: More than there is.

She kisses him. He retreats.

PAL: Wait, this isn't right…

REEMA: Sorry…I just…

They behold one another. She kisses him again. This time he responds. Lights slowly go down.

SCENE FOUR (NOVEMBER)

JEETO sits on her DFS chair. Her tabard and bag are by her side, her feet are soaking in a basin of water. Beside her, is the photo of her husband. She starts singing 'Mohabbat khi Jhooti' ['the lie that is love' – a famous hindi song] to the photo. PAL enters, takes out his iPad.

He's about to start typing but pauses. Finds a bottle of Johnnie Walker, opens it, pours himself a large tumbler of whisky. JEETO observes her son, puts the photo back in her bag.

JEETO: You used to want chah when you came home.

PAL: Uncle Manjit, he's doing my head in.

He swigs as he talks. Speaks quickly, almost to himself.

PAL: Sub-contractor's ready to fit the alarm system, but the Indian won't approve the overspend. Wants to know why we're so over budget. We've told him, it's cos the electrics were fucked and okay it's taken a few months, but it's sorted now. He keeps asking for the paperwork but we sent it ages ago. He's holding everything up and it's costing money. *(Pours another drink.)* Are you listening?

JEETO: Oh yes.

PAL: I mean there's gonna be setbacks, when you're doing, planning something on this scale…I've told Major. He thought he'd be starting next week…but he has to wait. Cookie's been kicking off saying he's bought the stock but what can I do?

JEETO: Harj's uncle is your boss.

PAL: He's not my boss, he's our partner.

JEETO: He has the biggest share.

PAL: Only cos there's no money in this fucking country. *(Swigs.)* And you, you're not exactly helping.

JEETO: Me?

PAL: You and Chacha sitting on that land, holding onto three hundred grand that's not doing anything…

JEETO: Don't talk about my land.

JEETO starts drying her legs, puts her shoes and socks back on. PAL glances over to the kitchen area.

PAL: I'll have me chah now. Where's Reema?

JEETO: Reema is not a Kenwood Teasmade. You make the chah.

PAL: I can't make it like you lot make it can I?

He reluctantly fills a saucepan with water. Puts it on the hob and throws cinnamon, cardamom and a tea bag into the water. MAJOR and COOKIE enter with shopping bags.

JEETO: Chah?

MAJOR: Yeah go on Mum.

JEETO: Cookie?

COOKIE: Alright.

PAL: How long's this water supposed to take?

JEETO comes over, takes over the tea.

COOKIE: *(Takes her coat off.)* You heard from the Indian?

PAL: I'm sorting it.

COOKIE: Major's bought half the stock already.

She starts unpacking the shopping. PAL opens his iPad.

MAJOR: Not half!

COOKIE: Nearly half, you've ordered it.

PAL: You can start in the next couple of weeks.

JEETO: *(To PAL.)* Your wife is upstairs.

PAL: What?

JEETO: Collecting the rest of her things.

PAL: Why didn't you say?

He goes to rush out.

JEETO: Leave her!

He carries on, she blocks his way.

JEETO: I said leave her. She is talking to Reema.

PAL takes this in. He retreats.

JEETO: She'll come when she's ready. She is packing the rest of her things.

MAJOR: Didn't see her car.

JEETO: Her father is outside waiting in his car.

MAJOR: We could have given her a lift.

COOKIE: Yeah, her mum and dad are only up the road. We see them in Asda all the time. They never say hello.

MAJOR: Did she take her car when she went?

COOKIE: Course she did. It's her car isn't it?

MAJOR: *(To PAL.)* Stock's in the warehouse. No need to worry about the stock.

JEETO gives out the tea. COOKIE eyes PAL.

COOKIE: If you don't get a move on your grand opening's gonna be delayed. I've booked that Channi from Alaap.

MAJOR: I used to like him.

They drink their tea. JEETO dishes out biscuits. They eat the biscuits. COOKIE opens the last carrier bag.

COOKIE: What do you think? For Chacha.

She holds up a couple of shirts.

MAJOR: Not bad.

COOKIE: You'll miss it Mum.

JEETO: Kee? *[What?]*

COOKIE: Pal's opening. Got your plane ticket haven't you? You'll be sitting on Chacha's verandah staring at your green fields.

JEETO: I'm not going.

COOKIE: But I've bought these now!

PAL: I knew it.

JEETO: What did you know?

PAL: You go on about leaving and then you change your mind. Same as all the other times.

JEETO: This is different from the other times.

PAL: Five hundred quid down the drain, how stupid can you get!

JEETO: Remember who you are talking to!

PAL: Five hundred Mum!

MAJOR: Why Mum?

JEETO: Reema.

COOKIE: What about her?

JEETO: Says she is ill.

MAJOR: Eh?

JEETO: You haven't noticed? Pal?

PAL: No.

JEETO: Because you don't speak to her any more.

PAL: I'm hardly here am I? I'm busy.

JEETO: Always bastard busy.

COOKIE: What's wrong with her?

JEETO: She thinks she has been poisoned.

MAJOR: Poisoned?

JEETO: Says she has eaten bad food. Every day she lies in bed moaning, groaning…I force her to come downstairs and eat toast.

She turns to stare at PAL.

JEETO: You know that kureeh brought so many shalwar kameez from back home. All twenty-one suits from her wedding day. None of them fit her any more. Too tight. *(Slaps her own stomach.)* Here.

PAL: *(Light/Nervous.)* She wants to go on a diet.

JEETO: I have been watching her. *(A beat.)* Her shape is changing.

PAL: What you telling us for?

JEETO: Maybe you know why?

JEETO stares at PAL. Suddenly slaps him round the face. He keels over.

PAL: It was a mistake. One mistake…

COOKIE: Bloody hell!

MAJOR: So are you and her like…

PAL: No! It was only once, wish I'd never laid eyes on her. Mum…

JEETO has her back to PAL.

JEETO: I don't want to look at your face.

PAL: Don't say anything to Liz.

COOKIE: *(To PAL.)* You stupid idiot.

PAL: I'm begging you, please…

COOKIE: Why can't you think before…?

MAJOR: Leave him…

COOKIE: …before you spoil things…

JEETO gathers her things together.

MAJOR: I said leave him!

COOKIE: And she's keeping it?

JEETO: She has no choice.

Silence. JEETO exits.

MAJOR: *(Sits down.)* Lot to take in this, isn't it?

A shocked PAL slowly composes himself. He goes to pour another drink.

COOKIE: You are unbelievable!

MAJOR: *(To COOKIE.)* You never made a mistake?

COOKIE: Not one this fucking stupid.

PAL: Nothing works without Liz.

MAJOR: *(To PAL.)* If you let her go now, give it some time, you never know, maybe she'll come back.

COOKIE: Don't give him hope. He doesn't deserve hope.

The door opens. LIZ enters. She's made up and smartly dressed, wearing an autumn coat. She holds a small suitcase. They stare at her.

MAJOR: Alright Liz.

LIZ: Alright Major.

COOKIE: How's your mum and dad?

LIZ: The same.

COOKIE: Do you want chah?

LIZ: No. Thanks.

She contemplates the space, walks over to the kitchen.

LIZ: It's been weird without me kitchen. *(Opens a cupboard.)* Oh, Mum's out of atta.

COOKIE: I'll get some.

LIZ: My mum and dad haven't got a thuva *[special roti pan]. (A beat.)* I'll have to buy one.

COOKIE finds the thuva under the cooker.

COOKIE: Take it.

LIZ: No I can't.

COOKIE: Go on, you have to have your roti.

LIZ takes it, puts it on the side. She observes the kitchen.

LIZ: I'm glad we got these units. They were pricey but they're so spacious. Me and Mum picked them out, just before our wedding wasn't it Pal?

PAL: Yeah.

LIZ: *(Picturing the memory.)* We sat on them thrones for the sagan *[blessing].* Like Posh and Becks. Remember?

PAL: Course.

LIZ: We got twenty grand that day.

MAJOR: Twenty?

LIZ: Yeah.

MAJOR: *(To COOKIE.)* How much did we get?

COOKIE: Six.

MAJOR: Did alright didn't you?

PAL: *(Gets up.)* Liz…

LIZ: *(Interrupts.)* My dad said they should have kept the Asian kids separate from us at school, on the other side of the classroom, you know like the men and women are at the Gurdwara. *(A beat.)* But no one could keep us apart.

PAL: Never.

LIZ: I turned my back on my family for you.

PAL: I know.

LIZ: I learned to goon the atta, make tharka, do gidha with Mum. Daddy always said I was more Indian than you. *(A beat.)* Can I please have a photo of him?

COOKIE finds one on the sideboard, hands it to her. LIZ looks at it.

LIZ: I still miss him so much.

PAL: I know.

LIZ: Take care of Mum.

PAL: I don't want this. Please…

Emotion rises in LIZ.

LIZ: All the years we've been trying, and it happened for you and her…just like that…

REEMA enters followed by JEETO who is holding a blanket. REEMA has put on weight but looks washed out. She and LIZ eye one another uneasily.

LIZ composes herself.

LIZ: At moments like this, you realise… There really isn't a God.

LIZ turns to JEETO and touches her feet. She picks up the thuva and exits. The front door slams. Moments pass. PAL runs out after her. JEETO helps REEMA onto the chair, she covers her with a blanket. JEETO gets a glass of water and tablets.

JEETO: Chah?

COOKIE: Not for me.

MAJOR: I'll have another cup Mum. *(To REEMA.)* So…er…how are you feeling?

REEMA: Not good.

JEETO hands REEMA a glass of water and some pills.

JEETO: Take these.

JEETO puts more chah on the hob. PAL returns, he goes to pour a whisky. REEMA takes the tablets.

COOKIE: What are they for?

JEETO: She feels sick. All the time.

COOKIE: It's called something, when you're sick the whole time…

MAJOR: What, until you have the baby?

COOKIE: Yeah.

PAL points at REEMA, he's getting drunk.

PAL: She should be the one going.

REEMA: I am ready to face my shame. Let it torture me. Liz was my friend.

COOKIE: Friend?

REEMA: This thing inside me, this sickness, it's like a poison, yes that's it…a poison inside…destroying my whole body.

PAL: *(To JEETO.)* Her staying here's wrong.

JEETO: *(Shouts.)* She's staying! This is because of your wrong, remember? *(A beat.)* Cookie chah bunah. *[make the tea.]*

COOKIE takes over the tea. She serves MAJOR and REEMA.

JEETO: *(To PAL.)* I'll tell you how things are going to be.

She goes over to the kitchen area, pours his drink into the sink.

PAL: What are you doing?

JEETO then pours the rest of the bottle down the sink.

PAL: Mum!

She opens a cupboard, finds another bottle of whisky. He tries to get it off her, they struggle. MAJOR and COOKIE rush over.

MAJOR: Bloody hell Pal!

COOKIE: Stop it!

PAL is about to take the bottle from her when MAJOR drags him away.

JEETO holds up the bottle.

JEETO: *(Breathless.)* You put this down.

> *She pours the rest of the bottle down the sink. JEETO hurriedly finds PAL's work bag, opens it, produces his iPad, hands it to him.*

JEETO: You take this thing, you go to work, you make that bloody nursing home into something. And then you wait for your child.

REEMA: If I'd found out before I could have got the poison out of my body.

JEETO: Choop kurreeh! *(To PAL.)* Something in this house has died, you killed it. And now a new time is coming.

PAL: I don't want it.

> *JEETO indicates REEMA.*

JEETO: You don't have to share a bedroom.

PAL: I can't do this.

JEETO: *(Fury rising.)* You think I'm going to fall down after standing tall all these years? After being spat at by goreh and now pitied by my own people. You think I'm going to let you turn me into nothing? *(A beat.)* Now go to work. Go to work. Jah. *[Go.]*

> *Dishevelled PAL slowly composes himself. He gathers his iPad and other stuff together, walks out. JEETO pours tea into two cups, puts a couple of slices of bread in a toaster. Hands one cup to REEMA.*

JEETO: Toast is nearly ready.

REEMA: I feel too sick.

JEETO: *(To COOKIE.)* Make sure she eats it.

> *JEETO heads out. COOKIE goes to stand by the toaster.*

REEMA: I should never have come to this house.

COOKIE: That's a no-brainer. *(Takes out butter and a knife/To MAJOR.)* This is more Liz's home than Pal's, but he's still here.

MAJOR: It was her choice to go.

Toast springs up, she starts buttering it.

COOKIE: He should suffer for this.

MAJOR: *(A beat.)* And what should happen to you?

COOKIE: Eh?

MAJOR: You're worse than your brother cos you pretend to be something you've never been. And I'm as bad.

COOKIE: Major…

MAJOR: I let you pretend, cos I wanted to believe in you.

COOKIE: Nothing's ever happened…I mean I've never done anything…I swear…

MAJOR: It's in your head all the time though, isn't it? *(Loud.)* Isn't it?

She nods.

MAJOR: You don't deserve the life you've got.

He exits. Shocked COOKIE watches him go. She looks at REEMA who has not touched her toast.

COOKIE: Maybe you'll be the mothering type. Wish I was, but I wasn't.

REEMA: I was drunk that night.

COOKIE: You must have been to have fucked Pal. *(Indicates toast.)* Mum said you have to eat that.

REEMA shakes her head.

COOKIE: Eat it!

Nothing. COOKIE takes the toast and angrily forces it into REEMA's mouth. She resists, chokes and gags. They struggle and REEMA finally succumbs to chewing it.

COOKIE: I'm sorry but you have to.

An upset REEMA slowly eats the toast.

SCENE FIVE

Months later. Spring. The living area is adorned with blue baby stuff. Cards and flowers are on all the tables and in the kitchen area. A bouncer and changing mat are on the floor. JEETO puts sheets in a moses basket. She glances towards the photo of her husband which is placed prominently on a decorative table.

JEETO: *(Excited/To photo.)* Soon you will see him properly.

> *She holds up a blue baby gro.*

JEETO: Five pounds in Asda. Binder was there, buying her lottery ticket. That dungar *[cow]* said to me, Bhanji, what is this kismet God has given you? I looked her straight in her small eye and I said God has given me a pottha *[grandson]*. If I die today my kismet has been more golden than I could have dreamed.

> *She goes over to the kitchen area and stirs a huge pot on the hob.*

JEETO: How can there be shame in a baby? So new and perfect and untouched. *(To photo.)* He looks like you.

> *PAL enters, sees all the baby stuff.*

PAL: Why's all the stuff down here?

JEETO: He is coming soon.

PAL: It's supposed to be upstairs. What's that smell?

JEETO: Panjiri. Atta, badam, ghee cooked up with sugar and more nuts.

PAL: I'll have some with me chah.

JEETO: It's for that kurreeh *[girl]*. If she eats it three times a day her milk will be rich and thick.

PAL: Might just have the chah.

> *He puts a pan of water on.*

JEETO: If only Daddy could hold him in his arms.

PAL: He'd probably get pissed and drop him.

JEETO: Choop kar *[Be quiet]*. That boy is your future.

> *PAL takes his iPad out.*

PAL: Here's the latest photos.

JEETO: *(Looks at the iPad.)* Bathrooms. Acha. Why so small?

PAL: Regulation spec!

JEETO: For a nursing home or a nursery?

PAL: Our Major's done a good job. And Harj reckons we're on track to open in eight weeks.

JEETO makes the chah.

JEETO: I thought we could go to the Gurdwara tomorrow.

PAL: What for?

JEETO: My grandson must have a name! The Giani will open the book and choose the letter. I have been praying for a G.

PAL: G?

JEETO: Gurgaggandeep Singh!

PAL: Bit long innit.

JEETO: My grandson needs something with impact.

JEETO receives a text, checks it, beams.

JEETO: Cookie…they are on their way.

PAL picks up his iPad, heads out.

JEETO: Where are you going?

PAL: Got work to do. I'll have me chah later.

JEETO: Aren't you going to greet him?

PAL: You're the one who wanted this Mum.

He continues out.

JEETO: I phoned Chacha.

PAL stops.

JEETO: He sends you budhaiya *[congratulations]*.

PAL: What have you told him?

JEETO: That you and Liz have a son. Why break one more heart?

PAL: You're mad.

JEETO: The boy is your blood.

PAL: I told you, she can stay here, and you can do what you want, but this is nothing to do with me.

JEETO: Then why do you care what I tell people?

PAL: Because it's a pack of lies! Chacha's gonna find out soon enough. Someone in the pind'll spread the gossip.

JEETO: Chacha will pretend it's not true.

PAL: What if he asks you?

JEETO: He won't.

JEETO pours out chah.

JEETO: We were talking the day he was born. He said now you have a son, things have changed.

PAL: What things?

She hands him papers from her bag.

JEETO: We both agreed it is time I put my land in your name.

PAL: You joking?

JEETO: Remember all the times you begged me for that land. Now you have shown me you can work like a dog, and suffer and suffer. You have earned it.

PAL: My business is what I've worked for. That land, your land, means nothing to me.

JEETO: It might to your son.

PAL: No. You keep it.

JEETO: Chacha sent all the papers weeks ago. *(Shows him.)* He was hoping for a boy. Please.

PAL: Why?

JEETO: It's the only thing Daddy can give him.

PAL looks through the papers.

JEETO: Sign, before he comes home. I want your daddy's heir to feel the power of his birthright when he comes through that door.

PAL signs the papers. JEETO puts them on the dining table.

JEETO: Now you have everything you wanted, this house, your business, your land, yes sir!

PAL: I still miss her Mum…

JEETO: Maybe next year we will all go to visit Chacha, take little Gurgaggandeep to visit your land…

PAL: I mean Liz…

JEETO: He will be walking by then, running! And his ticket is free until he is two. So we should go. We must!

PAL: Will you listen?

JEETO: I'm not interested in your memories!

COOKIE enters. She carries shopping bags and a car seat in which a baby boy sleeps.

COOKIE: Here's our little man!

She puts the seat down so the back faces the audience. JEETO is immediately flustered.

JEETO: Thail! *[oil!]* Where is it?

She covers her head with her chooni [scarf], rushes into the kitchen and pours a small amount of oil from a bottle of mustard oil into a bowl.

JEETO: Pani Barr mundhi dhee mayi, Sookha sookeh dhee noo ahah dhin aya *[Pour the water, boy's grandmother, the greatest comfort has arrived on this day]*

JEETO pours the oil down the frame of the door.

JEETO: Sagan *[blessing]* for my boy!

REEMA enters. She slowly sits down on the leather chair. She appears blank and uncomfortable. JEETO and COOKIE beam at the baby.

JEETO: Daddy number 2!

COOKIE: Spitting image.

PAL: Where's Major?

COOKIE: Gone back to your bathrooms, but he's been singing to him all morning. *(To baby.)* Hasn't he? Been singing? *(Chants.)* United! United! United!... Oh look he's smiling...

PAL: He's not.

JEETO: He is, he is. Smiling!

COOKIE/JEETO: United! United! United!

COOKIE: Major's already got him a football kit. Oh and I got him these.

She starts opening the shopping bags, takes out assorted baby clothes. JEETO squeals with joy. COOKIE holds up shorts and sunglasses.

COOKIE: For when he goes on holiday!

She holds up a tiny suit and tie.

JEETO: For when he goes to his office!

PAL: How much stuff does he need?

COOKIE: Shut yer mouth you!

In the kitchen area, JEETO puts Panjiri into a bowl.

COOKIE: I never appreciated Simmy and Jasmin when they were born. They just got on my nerves! I'm gonna make sure I enjoy my nephew!

JEETO: Nee kurrih.

JEETO hands the panjiri to REEMA. REEMA takes the bowl, starts eating with a spoon.

JEETO: Cookie, chah bunah.

COOKIE goes to make tea, JEETO goes to take the baby out of the car seat.

PAL: What you taking him out for?

JEETO: Choop kar *[be quiet].*

PAL beholds REEMA awkwardly.

PAL: *(To REEMA.)* Are you alright?

No response. JEETO sings a boli [traditional song] to the baby. She dances a gidha [dance] as she sings.

JEETO: We'll go to the Gurdwara with him tomorrow kurreeh, to name him. What do you think?

REEMA: He'll need a name.

PAL's phone rings. He answers it.

PAL: Harj. What?... Yeah... When?... How come?

PAL picks up his iPad, heads upstairs.

JEETO: Cookie, give her chah.

COOKIE hands REEMA a cup of tea.

JEETO: Okay Kurreeh?

REEMA nods.

JEETO: When did you feed him?

REEMA: Before we left the hospital. It hurt a lot. I'm sore, nearly bleeding. They said I could give him formula in the bottles.

JEETO: Hurt is normal. My grandson wants his mother's dhood *[milk].*

(To BABY.) Do you want to see your house? Come, I'll show you your room...

She exits.

COOKIE: Give him a bottle if you like. I got you some powdered.

COOKIE unpacks it and puts it in the kitchen.

COOKIE: A little baby, makes you feel so hopeful. Like a new chance to get things right. You did well, with the pushing, you forget how bad it is.

REEMA: I hated it.

COOKIE: *(Nostalgic.)* Like being hit on the back with a lawnmower, again and again...

REEMA: The whole thing was...disgusting.

COOKIE: Have your chah.

COOKIE watches her as she drinks.

COOKIE: You'll have to get down them baby groups. Singing nursery rhymes and comparing dirty nappies. That'll cheer you up. *(She starts making a bottle.)* Mum'll help, and I will. Pal's home'll be open soon. Get involved again and you'll be rich.

Suddenly MAJOR bursts in.

MAJOR: Where's Pal?

COOKIE: Major?

MAJOR: Where the fuck is he?

COOKIE: Upstairs.

MAJOR opens the door.

MAJOR: *(Shouts.)* Pal! Get down here!

COOKIE: What the hell's wrong?

MAJOR: Pal!

He paces around, he's a bag of nerves.

MAJOR: Fuck, fuck!

A shocked PAL enters.

PAL: I just heard…

MAJOR: You bastard.

PAL: I didn't know, I swear…

MAJOR grabs him.

MAJOR: All the blokes who work for me, their families…they trust me, I've let them down, because of you…

COOKIE: Major, get off him!

She comes between them.

PAL: It's gonna be alright.

MAJOR: Fuck off.

COOKIE: Will you calm down? What's happened?

MAJOR retreats.

MAJOR: The payment for the plumbing and the fittings. *(He can't say it.)* Your cheque's bounced…

COOKIE: Right, well…sometimes it happens…

MAJOR: Accountant just rang me.

PAL: I'm sorting it.

COOKIE: *(To PAL.)* I mean it's just cash flow isn't it?

PAL: *(Agitated.)* Uncle Manjit never paid the second instalment.

COOKIE: What?

PAL: Told Harj he's still missing the paperwork. *(To REEMA.)* But we sent it ages ago, didn't we?

REEMA: I don't know.

PAL: What do you mean? I told you to…

REEMA: I must have…forgotten.

PAL: *(Shouts.)* You were supposed to send it!

COOKIE: Get it to him now and then he'll release the money.

PAL: *(Shakes his head.)* He's pulled out.

COOKIE: What?

PAL: And…and the bank are calling in the loan.

COOKIE: No, no…they can't be…

MAJOR: *(To COOKIE.)* So he can't pay anyone.

PAL: I'll fix it. Once I've spoken to the bank.

MAJOR: I spent tens of thousands on stock. What about our mortgage? The girls' future?

PAL: I ain't gonna let anything happen to you am I? Not to my sister, my nieces…

MAJOR: My dad spent half his life breathing in asbestos so he could leave me that business, you ain't gonna destroy it…

COOKIE: Course he won't. He said he's gonna sort it. Aren't you Pal?

PAL: *(To MAJOR.)* Yeah, once the bank visit the premises and see how close we are, it'll be alright. I'll convince them. I will…

COOKIE: Well go on then. *(Urgent.)* Go on!

PAL takes out his phone. Presses a button. MAJOR and COOKIE watch him. REEMA picks up the papers PAL signed for JEETO. Lights fade.

SCENE SIX

Weeks later. The once immaculate living area is a mess. Dirty dishes are piled up by the sink. The room now appears dated and drab, as if it's in need of a lick of paint. An exhausted looking REEMA wears baggy cheap sportswear. She sits blankly. JEETO comes in from work. She glares at REEMA, hands her a dummy.

JEETO: I said I don't want you giving him a dummy.

REEMA contemplates the dummy. JEETO takes off her coat.

JEETO: You should have tried longer with your own milk. *(A beat.)* Did Pal do the phone call?

REEMA: Not yet.

JEETO: *(Sits down.)* Did he take you to the Town Hall?

REEMA: I forgot to tell him.

JEETO: What have you been doing all day?

REEMA: I don't know.

JEETO: My grandson needs his father's name on his birth certificate.

REEMA: Maybe his father should give him his milk.

JEETO: What's wrong with you Kurreeh?

REEMA: I don't feel like myself today.

JEETO: This is your kismet. Plenty of girls have it worse.

REEMA: Plenty.

JEETO: Once this money business is finished, we'll go to India, visit Chacha. I already told him you are good with the baby. I said you are better than Liz.

REEMA: You shouldn't have said that.

JEETO: I have to prepare him, for what is to come.

REEMA: What is to come?

JEETO: When the time is right, I will tell him Liz has gone and that you are to be the mother. And you both need to start thinking about a wedding.

REEMA: Wedding?

JEETO: Someone has to wipe up this mess. *(A beat.)* Sometimes Kurreeh you just have to endure. Find a way of tolerating. Look at me, I'm the one who told Pal to do that phone call. You think I want that to happen. Do you?

REEMA shakes her head.

JEETO: Make sure you both go to the Town Hall tomorrow.

A dishevelled PAL enters. He goes to the kitchen area, starts making tea. JEETO joins him, starts making a bottle of formula.

JEETO: Time for your boy's dhood.

PAL: Can't anyone round here fill a dishwasher?

REEMA: I haven't had time.

JEETO: He's going to be big and strong…

PAL: Doesn't take long.

He starts filling the dishwasher.

JEETO: …like his Dhadha.

PAL finds empty biscuit wrappers.

PAL: You've got time to eat custard creams.

JEETO: Did you help Harj move?

PAL: Yeah. He hasn't even got that much stuff left, he's sold nearly everything. Never thought he'd be living back with his mum and dad.

JEETO: You never left yours.

PAL: That was my mistake. *(Indicates REEMA.)* Her coming over was yours.

JEETO: Don't blame her.

PAL: She sits there all day, doing nothing.

JEETO: She's depressed.

PAL: Who isn't?

JEETO: Once you speak to this man, you can pay Major, pay all your debts?

PAL: Yeah.

JEETO: Thank God, we've still got this house.

PAL: It's all we've got.

JEETO: When is he calling?

PAL: In a few minutes.

JEETO: Tell me his name.

PAL: Jarnail Singh.

JEETO: Atwal?

PAL: Yeah.

JEETO: Mohinder's son. They used to rent land from Chacha. You must know him Reema.

REEMA: Yes.

JEETO: How can that cunjar afford my land?

PAL: He's made it big. Runs a dairy outside Ludhiana.

REEMA: He's a thief.

PAL starts to pace around.

PAL: If we'd had more time we could have found another investor. Harj even said so. Bank should have trusted us Mum. I hate this fucking country. You can't do anything here. We were trying to think big, take a risk…be brave…

JEETO: *(Flat.)* You didn't have the money.

PAL: My nursing home's standing there empty. Fucking repossessed! Half finished. Nearly finished. Some fucker's gonna come and take it over and all the blood and sweat we put in…was all for nothing. They're gonna take my business, my place…

JEETO: Stop this moaning, groaning.

PAL: It's not right.

JEETO: Is it right that I have to sacrifice my land to keep this roof over our head?

PAL: *(Angry.)* Don't you think I'm ashamed?

JEETO: *(Furious.)* Don't you say that. Don't you let anyone hear you say that! I bear the shame on my shoulders because you are my blood and that boy is your blood. You bear it. You live with your shame and you sell my land to Jarnail Singh Atwal. You do the right thing for this khandan *[family]*. Pay your debts and we'll live on roti *[bread]* and dayhee *[yoghurt]* in this house. And one day we'll do something. We'll find something else.

The landline rings. They stare at it for a moment. PAL picks up the phone.

JEETO turns to PAL.

JEETO: You are the Sardar *[chief]* here now. Do what you have to do.

JEETO exits with the bottle of formula.

PAL: *(Into the phone.)* Hello. Yes. Okay. Five minutes. Tell him I'll be ready.

He puts the phone down. REEMA gets up and faces PAL.

REEMA: I've packed my bags.

PAL: What?

REEMA: I'm leaving.

PAL: You were gonna go before.

REEMA: This time it's real.

PAL: Where?

REEMA: Doesn't matter. *(A beat.)* She still loves you.

PAL: How do you know?

REEMA: If I leave, she might come back.

PAL: She ain't coming back.

REEMA: I need money, if I'm going.

PAL: Not much of that round here.

REEMA: Mr Atwal will pay you for the land. You could give me some.

PAL: Why would I do that?

REEMA: So we end this hell we are living.

PAL: No. No way.

REEMA: Then I'll still go. But I'll take my baby with me.

PAL contemplates all the baby stuff.

PAL: He…he belongs here.

REEMA: I can go anywhere, mothers in this country have rights. They get help.

PAL: You can't just walk out and take him.

REEMA: It's up to you.

PAL: You'll be okay. You're clever, you know about books and all that.

REEMA: My books don't mean anything any more. So…if you want him to stay…

She finds a piece of paper in her pocket. Gives it to him.

REEMA: I've written it all down.

PAL inspects the paper.

PAL: You've never seen this sort of cash.

REEMA: Maybe I will now.

PAL: I need every penny I'm getting.

REEMA: I won't be back.

PAL: And you'll leave the boy, just like that?

REEMA: I said I would didn't I? Please. I have to go.

PAL: When?

REEMA: Today. Mr Atwal will transfer the money over to you and you can put my share into my account.

She indicates the piece of paper.

REEMA: See. I've written it all down.

PAL: I don't get you.

REEMA: I want to start again. Like I was never born. Please let me. I made a mistake. So did you. You owe me. You know you owe me something.

PAL: So the money's what matters?

REEMA: No, but freedom in your country, real freedom, it costs.

PAL: Don't you care about your son?

REEMA: Don't you dare ask me that. You'll look after him. And so will Mum. *(A beat.)* Put my money in. And I'll go, nice, clean and simple.

PAL: What if I don't?

REEMA: I'll find someone who'll take him.

PAL: Someone?

REEMA: Rich women here like brown babies.

PAL: That kid's mine!

REEMA: But there's no certificate. We keep forgetting to go to the Town Hall you see.

PAL takes this in.

REEMA: Please. It's best. For everyone.

Silence. The phone rings. PAL lets it ring. REEMA exits. He takes out papers and looks through them. PAL picks up the phone. He's nervous as he speaks, becomes more tense as the conversation proceeds.

PAL: Hello... Hahnji... Yes...it is... Sat Siri Akal... Good to speak to you...yes, I've spoken to your associate many times... Yes Mr Atwal... Sorry... Uncleji...yes... It's a very fair sum...thank you...I've signed most of the papers, I was planning to scan them…and…of course, I'll send the hard copies as soon as possible…

REEMA comes back in with the baby.

PAL: My mother says Sat Siri Akal… Hahnji Uncleji…yes I have…nearly three months old now…we named him after my father… Avtar Singh…

REEMA puts the baby in its bouncer. She puts her coat on.

PAL: Well, once I sell this land, I can cover our debts… No sir… I'm hoping to build my business back up…you heard right sir…bad luck, some very bad luck… I'm trying to build a future for my son…absolutely sir…I want to be a good father and try to lead by example like my own father…direct transfer…right…yes… Hahnji…yes sir…my mother's explained to Chachaji that he can remain in the house.

REEMA picks the baby up, cradles it and waits, listening to PAL.

He's sure he's not selling his share… But there's nothing I can do… I'll see… No, he won't listen to me…that quickly?… I see… There's one thing Uncleji…

He stops. REEMA stares at her baby.

PAL: I need a bit more… *(Breathes.)* I need a bit more time…to tell you… I'm sorry…but…but, I've changed my mind. I understand Sir… I'm very sorry…

PAL puts the phone down, regards REEMA. He's breathless.

PAL: I can't sell that land. Not to Atwal. Not to anyone. It's my father's land you see. And it's going to be my son's land and Mum's going to go…and stay with Chacha, and he's been doing all that building work on the house and she keeps talking about staring at those green fields. It's all she wants, in her heart, and I can't deny her that… I won't… She deserves it.

REEMA eyes him. He scrunches up the papers, then turns to the kitchen cupboard, finds the biscuit jar, puts it on the table.

PAL: There's usually a couple of hundred in here. Have it if you want.

REEMA: You…you make sure you look after him…

After a few moments, she composes herself and hands PAL the baby. She opens the jar and frantically stuffs the money in her pockets. She exits. PAL is left with the baby in his arms.

SCENE SEVEN

The stage is transformed into a grubby, grim council flat. A vast expanse of space, bare and soulless. Someone left the dirty mattress they died on in a corner. Bits of litter here and there. Chintz curtains hang at the back, they are closed and cover a massive window. The layout of the space is the same as JEETO's house but the decor is a thousand times cheaper. The kitchen area is old-fashioned, modest. A suitcase and a black bag are on one side of the room. PAL and COOKIE enter through a door, with more black bags, a broom and cleaning materials. They put them next to the suitcase and black bag. COOKIE contemplates the space as PAL unpacks.

COOKIE: Tried not to look at it before.

She's almost in tears.

PAL: Stop it.

COOKIE: *(Composing herself.)* Can't bear the thought of you here.

PAL: The area's coming up.

COOKIE: A council flat Pal!

PAL: Ex-council, and we only just managed to afford it. Least I'm still a homeowner.

COOKIE: This isn't your home.

PAL: Course it is. Go and see, it's not so bad.

COOKIE disappears through the door. Once she's gone, PAL stops unpacking and beholds the room, he almost crumbles but holds it together. PAL removes kitchen utensils from a box, starts putting them away. COOKIE returns.

COOKIE: Her shalwars won't fit into that bedroom never mind the kameezes.

She picks up litter, starts sweeping up.

COOKIE: You can use our garage for storage.

PAL: We're lucky to have a place at all.

COOKIE gets a text.

PAL: Tracey?

COOKIE: No, er…me and Tracey aren't in contact any more.

PAL: How come?

COOKIE: Thought we were close, but really, we hardly knew each other. Fact is, she was a boring old cow. *(Texts back.)* Major says Mum's on her way, but he's staying downstairs.

PAL: What for?

COOKIE: Doesn't wanna leave the car.

PAL: Why?

COOKIE: He's not risking his laptop!

PAL: Tell him to bring it.

COOKIE: There's a gang out there!

PAL: Two kids playing football on the green bit! Mum's coming up on her own isn't she?

COOKIE: Well he's watching her, from the car isn't he?

PAL: *(Unpacking.)* Did he get that conversion job?

COOKIE: Yeah, and he's doing up those flats in Broad Green an' all. We've been lucky.

PAL: Yeah.

COOKIE: You know, he admires you, for what you did. We both do.

PAL: Right.

COOKIE: Think you're stupid. But we admire you.

JEETO enters with the baby in its car seat. She puts the baby to the side of the room. COOKIE feigns enthusiasm.

COOKIE: Bedrooms are nice! Bigger than you'd think! And you know Major's gonna sort out that kitchen, and the bathroom…

JEETO: Sabkoosh hohjooga. *[Everything will get done.]*

COOKIE: And me and the girls can hold a paintbrush.

JEETO takes out the photo of her husband, balances it on a kitchen surface [facing away from the audience]. She regards it for a moment then starts cleaning up in the kitchen. COOKIE receives another text.

COOKIE: I'd better go.

PAL: Don't you want chah?

PAL continues to unpack and JEETO carries on cleaning as they talk.

COOKIE: Jasmine's in a swimming competition. We're all going to watch. We'll come round after. Bring some dinner.

PAL: Okay.

COOKIE: Do you want Nando's or Domino's?

PAL: I'm not bothered.

COOKIE: Mum, Nando's or Domino's?

JEETO: Kooshvee *[Whatever]*.

COOKIE: Mum, decide! Which one do you want more?

JEETO: I don't know.

COOKIE: Shall I get Nando's?

JEETO: Okay.

COOKIE: Or Domino's?

JEETO: Okay.

COOKIE: Mum!

PAL: Get what you lot want innit.

COOKIE turns to go. She stops, turns to JEETO.

COOKIE: Mum…

JEETO: Hah?

COOKIE: Come and stay with us.

JEETO: *(Cleaning.)* A woman does not live with her daughter.

COOKIE: Please…

JEETO: Choop kar *[Be quiet]*… This place is a palace compared to the kamara *[room]* me and Daddy used to have. God has given Pal another chance, today he is born again.

COOKIE: Nandos it is then.

She exits. PAL unpacks, eyes his mother.

PAL: Harj's dad offered me a job.

JEETO: Acha.

PAL: Managing one of his pound shops. Wants me to keep on top of the stock. Do the Cash and Carry runs and all that. Monday to Sunday. I've said yes.

JEETO: Good.

PAL: But me and Harj aren't letting go. We'll have our business, even if it's not the nursing home, we'll open a dry cleaner's or a take away or something. We'll have it.

JEETO: *(Cleaning/A beat.)* They were advertising cleaning shifts at the hospital.

PAL: *(Stops.)* You said never again.

JEETO: We say a lot of things.

PAL: I won't let you…

JEETO: I've already started. Last week. Before I do the tea trolley.

She eyes his dejected countenance.

JEETO: You change that face boy. Your son has a home and you have a job and I have two jobs. You try something, build your business and when you make your money, then…then I'll go back to my land.

They stare at each other for a moment. The baby is unsettled. PAL picks him up. JEETO carries on cleaning. PAL walks him around for a while, soothing him. Eventually the baby calms down and PAL ̇him up, just as JEETO previously described Daddy holding PAL ̇hen he was a baby.

PAL: *(Soft/To son.)* What you thinking Son? What you gonna be? Whatever the hell it is, you find your way. Find it... we'll be watching...

JEETO: Put his clothes in my kamara.

PAL: He'll be alright in with me. *(To baby.)* Come on, I'll show you round your house.

He heads out.

JEETO: Pal.

PAL: *(Stops.)* Yeah?

JEETO: God will reward you...for my land.

PAL: My land Mum.

He takes the baby, exits. JEETO finishes cleaning up and opens the curtains. The view is surprisingly pleasing and almost resembles the green fields she has been describing in the Punjab. She takes it in, laughs to herself, laughs and laughs until she wipes tears from her eyes. She then moves to the kitchen area, takes out a pan, puts it on the hob.

JEETO: *(Shouts.)* Pal, chah peeneeyeh? *[Do you want a cup of tea?]*

Lights down.

THE END